The Saga

of the

Muses

by
Willie L. Muse

The book cover was designed by Pronto Press, Inc.

Front Cover drawing by the Author, Rev. Dr. Willie L. Muse

Printed in the United States

Library of Congress-in-Publication Data

The Saga of the Muses

ISBN #978-0-9823607-0-5

Nonfiction Autobiography

Table of Contents

The Saga of the Muses

Acknowledgments

It is with a sense of deepest gratitude that I acknowledge the following for their dedicated and unselfish service in aiding me through the various aspects of making this book ready for publication: First, I owe a special debt of gratitude to my younger sister, **Mrs. Ida B. Henderson**, and **Mrs. Patricia Harper Echols**, a dear and devoted member of the Ebenezer Baptist Church of Auburn, Alabama, for the seemingly limitless hours that they spent scanning over my selection of words and correcting my poorly selected grammar, which often bordered between stiff colloquialism and unacceptable harshness, which at times reflected a period of life that they could not have possibly understood being so young.

Then I am grateful to my daughter, **Ms Linda D Muse**, for her many hours of technical assistance in setting up the computer and serving as a sounding board for me as I struggled to include or delete certain materials from these writings.

Finally, my sincere and deepest appreciation goes to the many members of the **Ebenezer Missionary Baptist Church**, Auburn, Alabama, along with some local **pastors** and **friends** of the Auburn community for their patience and tolerance they exhibited by returning to the church on a busy Sunday evening to listen to the reading of the first six completed chapters of this book. Their comments and encouragement were simply over whelming. As well as for my **children** and **siblings,** several of whom were old enough to bring to memory certain experiences that I had long since laid to rest in the backroom of my mind.

This book is honorably and respectively dedicated to
The sacred and cherished memories of our dear departed mother, **Mrs. Mattie Muse Houston,** who despite our lives of abject poverty, was able to forge out of it a family of integrity and high values. And of course, no memory or reflection on the history of my life would be complete without mentioning my old saintly departed great grandmother, **Mrs. Hattie Muse,** affectionately known by all who knew her as **Mommy Lillie.**

And finally to My dear and beloved wife **Mamie Ruth,** who supported me in this endeavor, and made it possible by creating and maintaining an atmosphere that was conducive for concentrating and writing during the many long hours that it took to produce this book.

Author's Preface

The Muses' in Greek and Roman Mythology

According to Roman and Greek Mythology, the Muses were the goddesses of song and later of other arts and sciences. Originally they were said to have been nymphs but later they were usually represented as the daughters of Zeus and Mnemosyne, the personification of memory. As goddess of different arts and sciences, they were nine in number, with names, attributes and representing symbols by which they were known given as follow:

(1) Clio, history (a scroll);
(2) Euterpe, lyric poetry (flute);
(3) Calliope, epic poetry (wax tablet and stylus);
(4) Melpomene, tragedy (tragedy mask, ivy wreath and club of Heracles);
(5) Thalia, comedy and pastoral poetry (comic mask, ivy wreath, and shepherd's staff);
(6) Polyhymnia, sacred poetry (veiled with pensive attitude);
(7) Terpsichore, choral poetry and dance (lyre);
(8) Erato, love poetry (small lyre); and

The Saga of the Muses

(9)   Urania, astronomy (celestial globe).

It should also be noted that the modern name "Museum" derived from a Greek word which meant, "Seat of the Muses" (Collier's Encyclopedia Vol. 14, pp. 292A, 292 B, 1959)

We make no claim of any connection or relationship to these mythological deities, only the sharing of their name, which our fore parents somehow inherited from some unknown source. Our immediate family also shares their number of which there were nine of them and altogether, also there are nine of us. Apart from these there would be absolutely no reason to even mention them in this humble account of our family's history. However, we do make use of the scroll on our cover and the denotation of chapters of this book, which is the symbol of Clio, the goddess of history, which is undoubtedly the nature of these writings.

Chapter One

Those Earlier Impossible Years
1939 -1948

Having been born in 1935, It may seem somewhat strange, but I can remember as far back as two or three years of my life. My growing up in a very large family was indeed a most memorable experience, in addition to me and some of my younger siblings, there also others who lived with us in the home of our great grandmother, who in fact, became our grandmother figure, since her daughter, our real grandmother died before I was old enough to know her. Our great grandfather also had passed away when I was about three years old. My mother and her husband of a few years had separated. We went back home to live with Mama Lillie, Pa Dad and another single aunt who was also living there with four of her children. Additionally, there was a younger brother and sister of my mother whose mother (my grandmother) died while they were baby and knee baby. These two children would become the responsibility of our mother to raise after the death of Mama

Lillie. Therefore, we were never short of having much company, and there was never a shortage of food for everyone. Although, some times it amounted to only milk and cornbread, both of which were grown on the farm where we lived.

The earliest memory that I have of my childhood was when I was three or four years of age, during the last days of our great grandfather, whom we called "Pa Daddy." I guess I remember this time mostly because Pa Dad's health was failing along with his sight. It was my responsibility to lead him by the hand around the house and yard, so that he wouldn't stumble over things and hurt himself. Of course he constantly blessed me for being eyes for him during this time. My mother's youngest sister, whose nick name was "Baby Sister" was a few months younger than me; she was always there to assist me in this task. Between the two of us, Pa Dad was well cared for, until one day when he had to use the bed pan, I said to her, "Baby Sister, when Pa Dad finishes, you will have to take it out, for it will be too heavy for me." Of course, my mother, (unknown to me) heard me. After a few lashes with a switch, my mother made this a permanent chore of mine until his condition got to the point that an adult had to be constantly at his bed side. That was the case until he died several months later.

Pa Dad's death was my first experience with death. For up to that time I cannot remember ever even having any thought of it. There were some who knew him who said that he predicted the process of his death. They say that he told them he would sleep for four days and then he would go to heaven. I do remember how he was in a coma in his bed room for many days. The exact number of days I can't remember, but he laid in a deep sleep snoring with his mouth open, until the last day when he seemed to have awakened briefly. He then turned over, and was gone.

The time of the funeral was an entirely different experience for the rest of the children and me, being so young, none of us had the slightest idea of even the meaning of the word, "funeral". We only knew that there was an eerie hush around the house during that time. The usual laugher that was almost always heard around the house, especially during the evening, when the day was over and all the chores were done, was reduced to quiet muffled whispers. The men of the plantation gathered to bathe and dress the body in preparation for the burial, (Even though embalming was an age-old art, it was not even thought of as a practice on the plantation at that time.) The women gathered to bring dishes of prepared foods, as they attempted to console Mama Lillie and the family, while they talked about what a great man Pa Daddy was.

After the men had finished their sacred task of bathing and dressing the body, a mule drawn wagon crept slowly toward the house driven by yet another man from the plantation, that wagon was bearing a cheap cloth covered casket, that probably cost no more than the wooden box that encased it. The men and women even worked by oil lamps, because the only house that had electricity was the "Big House." That was the house of the plantation owner. The barns and horse stables even had electricity but not the sharecroppers' shanties. The body was placed inside the casket and was laid out in the house on two straight chairs, one chair on each end of the casket facing each other. There it would lay all night until time for the funeral the next day.

The Day of the Funeral

Being so young at the time, I can't recall many details of the day of the funeral, such as whether there was a church funeral or just the graveside service. I can however, recall events that took place about the house. All the children had to take early morning tin tub baths, which was rather unusual since it was morning and not Saturday night, the usual tub bath night for the younger members, of the family, and occasionally, for some of the grownups as well. But this was just another of the strange occurrence that was taking place in our home which indeed baffled the minds of all the children, most of whom were too young to understand just what was going on at that time.

After our baths, each child was dressed in clean well-starched clothes. We often quietly walked past the casket as we moved from room to room in the process of getting dressed. By the time the grownups had finished dressing, the announcement was made that the truck had arrived. We were all rustled up and lifted up onto the long open body semi- truck, joining many other relatives and friends from the plantation, on the front of which the casket had already been placed. Mama Lillie and one of her sisters sat sternly in the cab with the driver of the truck. A few other vehicles accompanied us, as we moved slowly down the dusty road from the house to the cemetery some two or more miles away. A large crowd had already gathered when we arrived at the gravesite.

As kids, we were too excited about the ride on the truck to care very much about what else was going on around us. First, the truck itself, was exciting. To our young eyes it seemed to have been almost the size of a modern-day football field. This truck was used mainly to haul cotton to the gin or to carry cattle to the stockyard. It had wooden sides held together by two heavy metal chains that stretched from side to side across its huge body, one chain was near the front of the truck where the casket lay, and the other near the rear, with its live human cargo carefully seated or standing between the two of them. Then, there was the excitement of our riding so high off the ground with the dusty wind rushing swiftly upon our faces, roaring noisily passed our ears and tickling our freshly combed and brushed hair as if so many skilled fingers were making a frantic effort to soothe our sorrows and comfort our youthful hearts. Despite the occasion, this indeed would prove to be the most exciting and most memorable ride of my young life.

At the Graveside

Awaiting at the small tree strewn cemetery were several small groups of people, field hands, members from the Baptist church and other churches from the adjacent communities, relatives and friends of the family who had found some way to get to the gravesite other than by riding on the truck that had brought the body and us to the scene. Some had ridden on horse or mule back, some had come by mule drawn wagons or horse drawn buggies, some had walked on foot, and a very few had even come by shabby outdated automobiles or trucks, very few of which were owned by black people who lived somewhere in the distant neighborhoods. They all stood around talking in the same

5

hushed tone that had been heard about the house since the death of Pa Dad a few days ago. The plantation owner had also arrived with his wife and mother who remained in their car fanning with long wooden handle fans, while he moved busily about the freshly dug grave, as if he was directing the toss of every shovel of dirt that was scooped from the seemly bottomless pit called a grave.

As we all gathered behind the tall mounds of freshly dug dirt that was taken from the grave, we curiously watched as the men lay long poles across the grave on which they carefully placed the casket, above the wooden box that had already been placed in the grave. After a brief program consisting of songs, a prayer, a brief sermon by the pastor, and ended, with the plantation owner dropping a few coins briskly taken from his pocket into the grave, four men with ropes then gently let the casket down into the grave, and nailed the lid on the wooden box. Other men commenced to cover the grave with the dirt that had been taken up when the grave was dug, leaving a heap piled on top of it. And they placed two wooden stakes, one at the head and one at the foot of the grave, which turned out to be the only marker that ever indicated where Pa Dad was buried. After a few tears and sobs from family members, we were once again lifted onto the truck and slowly left the grave site for home, leaving Pa Dad behind all alone out doors all by himself for the first time ever. And just like that, he was gone, leaving us with only fading but fond memories of him.

Life around the house after the funeral was somewhat doleful and uneventful. The days seemed to be a steady humdrum of unbroken sadness for all the family and especially for Mama Lillie who seemed to have been at a terrible loss and sort of remained to herself for quite some time since the funeral. She spent her days walking about the house humming songs that were meaningless to us. We had often heard those songs in church meetings when she had taken Baby sister and me with her. It was always a very frightening experience for the both of us, since she always constantly talked back to the preacher and some times she even shouted, throwing her pocket book sending its contents flying in various directions. In those days, she also immersed herself in the rearing of her great grand-children, raising chickens, turkeys and even a few very noisy guinea fowls, their noisy chatter kept both fowls, animals and people awake all the days and most of the nights.

As time moved on, Mama Lillie slowly returned to her old self again. In addition to her interest in her chickens, turkeys and us, she became vitally interested in growing flowers and vegetables. While her vegetables were great and many, her flower garden was simply out of this world. For in this garden she grew many varieties of gorgeous flowers that seemed to include every color of the rainbow and some. She attended to this precious plot religiously, ridding it of even the smallest sprig of foreign weeds or grass. This made it an ideal place for me to hide and lie in wait to catch beautiful butterflies that constantly darted from flower to flower gathering the sweet nectar from the wide opened blossoms. I even yielded to the temptation to seal a bumblebee in an open bloom that was just above the place where I was crouched, only to learn that the business end of the bee, the stinger, was the end that was closest to my fingers. And of course, needless-to-say, this was a one time only act. After that I resumed catching butterflies and substituted catching Junebugs instead of bumblebees.

Having made a full comeback, Mama Lillie became known for three unique characteristics. First, she was known for her tidiness and cleanliness both inside and outside the house. As in those days when there were very few lawn mowers, (reel to reel push mower at that) she would make us shave the grass from the front yard with a hoe, rake it up and burn it. The back yard was always clear of grass scuffled clean by all the children constantly playing on it. She would then have us to make "brush brooms" from small sweet gum trees with which we had to sweep the yard at least once each week. We swept more often if it was the time of year when the several mulberry trees around the house were shedding their leaves, which they always produced super abundantly. At least two or three times a year, we would even have to crawl under the house and sweep beneath it. This of course, was the chore most dreaded by all of us children.

Secondly, she was known for the beautiful quilts that were almost always in the making. She would take scraps of cloth left over from some garment that she or some one else had made or discarded, and sew, or piece, them onto patterns cut from news papers or pieces of brown paper bags, which when sewed together formed the most beautiful, artistic and colorful designs ever placed on any bed.

Next was the quilting party where several women of the community would come and gather around the framed quilt hanging from the ceiling by strong cords or small ropes, and there they would quilt together most of the day and sometimes even into the night until a quilt was finished. We children had to always remain near to thread the needles for them as they ran out of thread. We were always being made to feel good and proud as they bragged about what good eyesight we youngsters had. Unquestionably her most joyful and proudest moments were on the days when she would hang all her completed quilts on clothe lines strung all around the house to sun or air them out, (or proudly show them off) as passersby would gaze and look admirably at them. Some of them even offering to buy some of them for themselves or some other relative or friend. Of course this was in most cases to no avail.

Lastly, she was known for the strict and firm disciplinarian characteristics which she held strong sway over all her children, even those who were all grown and gone to live else where, as well as all of her grand and great grand children, and even other children and sometimes, grownups that came around her from time to time. She would enforce her acts of discipline by either invoking the fear of God through her godly lectures, or by the fear of her gin belt which she kept under her mattress when it was not in use on us, or she would make use of one of the ever present "brush broom" which was made from small trees and used for sweeping the yard. She would often employ both when she disciplined us, as she would whip a while and talk a while, leading us children to call this capital punishment, for the whipping never hurt as much as the talk that went along with it.

1. Author's sketch of plantation home it was completely destroyed by fire shortly after the family moved to Montgomery.

Chapter 2

Members of the Family

The next few years there seemed to have been nothing of significance happening around the house, affording me the opportunity to reflect on other members of the family, those that lived in the house with us as well as those that frequently came by either to eat or just to visit as a daily ritual but lived elsewhere on the plantation, or they alternately lived with us and away at the same time.

There were our mother's four brothers, named in descending order, Russell, (Buck) Fred, (Dezo); James; and the youngest, Adam (Sport), who was a baby when their mother died. Then of course, there was my mother Mattie, called Tut and her sisters, Mary, who was called Honey and Eddie Mae, the younger sister whom we called Baby Sister, and Hattie, who was called Biddy, She was married and lived away with her family. It is quite obvious that the giving of nicknames was a common practice among our people on the farm at that time. Therefore, the nickname was more often used in reference to family members and acquaintances than their real names were.

Next were the children of our mother and her older sister Mary, all of whom played an important role in the overall makeup of our family household. They were always around and shared in performing the daily chores that we did from day to day about the house. In addition to myself, the oldest, my mother had two other sons during this time. The middle child died by the age of three, leaving only Nelson, my younger brother and me, her only two children at this time. Of course several more sisters and brothers would follow in the coming years.

Aunt Mary also had three sons, they were, Matthew (Man) her eldest, and perhaps the most colorful, who certainly merits a full chapter elsewhere in this family record. Then there was Ben, the middle son, and A Gee, the youngest, who was killed in an accident, while riding on the back of a truck loaded with horses during his early pre-teens. He had slipped away from home without his mother's consent - even in spite of her warning him against it - to attend a horse show in Selma. On the way back the truck ran off the road and he, along with a couple of horses was killed. Like our mother, her family too would increase with several more sons and daughters in the coming years.

Since I was so young and frail, older members seemed to be so big and strong forcing me to compare myself to them as a small shrubbery amidst tall timbers in a dense forest. My frailty was due to some strange and unknown illness that befell me and almost brought an end to my life at youth. I can remember to this day the awful fever, the bitterness that lingered in my mouth, and the excruciating pains and weakness that I experienced at that time. I also remember the daily visits to the doctor's office. It, a two-mile journey, was made mostly by foot during the coolest part of the day. Sometimes the boss man's wife, in her new and flashing car, gave us a lift. She was a rather kind and sympathetic woman, who even on some occasions would come back to take us home when our visit with the doctor was over.

It was during one of these visits that I heard the rather inconsiderate and often vulgar speaking doctor tell Mama Lillie, that since I was so sick and he did not know what was wrong with me, that she could only expect the worse at any time now. She asked, "You mean you think that he is going to die?" upon his affirming the fact, she told him, "Let me try another doctor who not only knows what is wrong with him but how to cure him as well." Although I was rather young and very sick, I was well enough to know that she was referring to Jesus Christ, with whom she seemed to always be in communication. She even shouted sometimes when the name of Jesus was mentioned whether she was in church or just walking with a friend who was returning home after a long visit with her at our home. They would constantly seesaw along the way while solving all the world's problems and they often shouted as they went. Eventually they would spin off for home going in different directions, bringing an end to yet another old-fashion country visit.

Whatever the case, her prayers for me seemed to have worked. I recovered so well that I never had to visit a doctor again, except for treatment for a foot injury that I received while cutting firewood. This injury requiring several stitches happened during my senior year in high school, which was many years after her death. Otherwise, I recovered so well that I never had to visit the doctor again. When I was drafted into the army some fifteen or twenty years later, upon receiving my medical records from my hometown doctor, I learned from them that he had listed that I had had an irrecoverable case of diphtheria fever. My cure then left me to conclude that Mama Lillie's prayers, coupled with time and daily doses of hated Cod-liver oil, had come to my rescue, by the power of God, with whom I came to know that all things are always possible.

Chapter 3

Glimpses of Better Days Ahead

Life seemed to move along in slow motion for the next several years with only routine happenings taking place month after month. Until finally, there was a buzz around the house about our going to school for the first time. This of course, brought on much excitement to all of us children, as several of us had reached school age around the same time. And none of us knew just what to expect as we prepared for our first day of school. I cannot recall as to whether or not the older children had attended before that time. If they had with my being so young, it certainly didn't mean anything to me anyway. But as for now everything is quite different. For, I am going to school.

This was indeed an exciting time around our house, as our mothers were busy planning and buying things that we needed for this great venture. They bought new clothes for every one, along with little square lunch boxes with handles and decorated with pictures of Red Ryder and Little Beaver, Roy Rogers and Trigger, or some other characters that were unknown to us since we were tucked so far away at the end of a dusty country road in the cotton field behind the woods. They bought us tablets with rough paper that reminded me of over-cooked corn bread, left for days in the sun to dry; and wooden pencils with over-size rubber erasures; along with little coloring books with a box of wax crayon, the first of which I had ever seen; They bought us little rain coats to keep us dry should we got caught in the rain that frequently seemed to come out of nowhere even on the brightest of days. Finally they bought us little book sachets to carry all this stuff in. In fact we had so many new things that the only thing to compare it with was, Christmas morning when some good willed pot-belly Santa Claus rewarded us for good behavior that we had done during the year, like picking up chips for firewood, and washing our feet without being told, before going to bed at night.

Chapter 4

Wow! School at Last

Finally, the long awaited day had come. We were awaken early in the morning and hurriedly dressed after eating an unwanted breakfast. We slowly moved about the house like half -sleep zombies, almost paralyzed with anticipation, bumping into each other as we put on our new clothes and shoes getting ready for the greatest venture yet of our child hood lives.

We were herded from the house by our mothers, as they swiftly walked with us taking a short cut through the often muddy, back wood wagon trail heading to the school house located on another road, which seemed to have been miles away, even though it would later proved to be a little more or less than a half mile from our house. Of course, I couldn't wait to get to school and get to the new stuff that was packed away in my book sachet. But it was the biscuit and jelly sandwiches and home made teacakes in my lunch box that really taunted me and tested my patience to its limit of endurance.

Marching like little toy soldiers, we approached the woods amidst the many noises that we had become so accustomed to hearing through-out the night and day, most of the year. However, they seemed to have been much louder than usual on that brisk fall morning as we neared the woods headed for school. There were the bellowing sound of what seemed to have been tens of thousands of bull frogs and many other kinds, some seemed to be singing bass while another thousand or so, smaller frogs, seemed to sing soprano or a hundred or more other musical notes and tones. Thus giving the forest a somewhat enchantment which I still seem to hear when I am out of doors and the wind is still and quiet around me.

(You may wonder just why I spend so much time describing these woods, marshes and ponds. It is because these woods, marshes and ponds are part of a recurring dream that I have had on a regular basic since I was a child even up to this present time. Just why, I don't know, they just seem to be a part of my life that will go with me to my grave I think. Maybe it is because often, even as a child, I had to wade into the grassy waters edge, ignoring the snakes and other slinking reptiles, to untangle the line or chain of a cow that had broken loose from its stake, and wandered in there in search for a drink of water or to graze on the tall grass that grew in the shallow marshes. We would always wade in with the voice of some grown-up ringing in our ears cautioning us to "Watch out for the snakes." Or may be it is because of a more pleasant experience that I enjoyed every summer of, picking huckleberries from the scrubby bushes that dotted the edge of the pond. In any rate, the same dream keeps coming back to me time and time again.)

In the distance we could hear the loud outburst of an often heard but seldom seen, Sage- hen cackling in the tall grasses near the pond and marsh land that was home for the frogs that sang, as well as snakes and other such creeping things. High over our heads a pair of noisy Chicken hawks glided swiftly through the sky as if they were singing a never-ending song and watching our every move from above, while the grown-ups did the same from among us. But what did we care about any of this today? We were on our way to school at last.

Coming out of the woods, we entered into a wide -open field beyond which we came to the churchyard and almost hidden behind the church was a one room weather-beaten grayish–black building that was somewhat leaning to one side. Some of the panes were broken out of the windows and were replaced with cardboard of various colors. Of course, that didn't bother us none since we didn't have windows with glass panes in our house any way. There was no porch before the door, so we stepped off the ground upon a little set of wooden steps right up into the building. What do you know? At the ripe old age of six, I had finally made it to school.

Once inside I couldn't help but notice the rows and rows of church pews that were spread from the front door to the rear that crowded the building. I remembered these pews as some of the same ones that Baby Sister and I had often sat on as we attended worship service with Mama Lillie, long before we were large enough for our little legs to hang down toward the floor. So I realized that they were taken out of the church next door.

Near the front and to the left side of the room stood a tall pot-belly heater, which to us was indeed a modern-day marvel, since all the heaters that we had ever known were narrow wood-burning fireplaces that heated each room in our house during even the coldest of winters; along with the cooking stove that heated the small kitchen that was detached from the rest of the house, and attached by a slanted ramp that often froze over in winter making the simple task of eating breakfast, a rather hazardous experience. This stove provided heat for us as meals were prepared from day to day for our rather large family.

Seated at a desk at the far end of the room, just in front of a freshly painted "black board" with oversize red lettered alphabets painted across the top, was a small round face, bright eyed lady, who was franticly working with mothers, one at a time, trying very hard to remain calm and pleasant even under a very stressful condition, as they attempted to register their restless and frightened children in school, many like us, were there for the very first time. Having completed our registering, we came to know this lady as, Miss Merlene Taylor, our elementary teacher, the first teacher that I ever had. And to whom I would very shortly become sort of a "teacher's pet" as later, she would from time to time, have me remain after school in order to present me to the PTA members as her " little one hundred boy."

Little did I know that this single event of being at school would become an intricate part of the rest of my life, (For, entering school for the first time at the age of six. Little did I know that I would be in school, off and on, for the next forty three years, getting my last degree at the age of forty-nine. I would be affiliated in some capacity of schoolwork from now on.) But of course, there was no way of knowing this, nor was I the slightest concern at this time, the only thing that mattered to me this day was, that I was finally in school. Therefore having to go to bed early at night and getting up so early in the morning was no dread at all to me. Furthermore, fighting the early morning chill only added to the excitement of my newfound adventure.

Days at school, for the most times were fast and filled with excitement. Since there was only one teacher to teach the four grades held at the school, for only grades primer through grade four were offered there at that time. — Although two other grades would be added with the building of a new two-room schoolhouse a few years later, which would replace the old building now reeking with time and age—Each class would take terms in reading, writing, spelling or arithmetic. They then would be given problems or other bookwork tasks to do while the teacher attended to the next class.

There was a marked advantage for us in having all classes in the same room, for the lower class often learned the lessons that were taught to the upper classes. There fore, by the time we were promoted to the next level, we almost always knew the lesson by heart. And the upper classmen also had the chance to review lessons that they may not have fully understood, as they observed lower classmen struggle with lessons that they had already passed.

My first classes seemed rather simple and somewhat silly to me, as one by one, we had to read, almost in singing fashion, verse after verse from a little thin paper book titled "Dick and Jane." Each of us had to stand before the teachers desk or near the pew on which we sat, and repeat the lesson that we had learned as our mothers carefully taught us before we washed our feet and went to bed the night before. The verses went like this:

The Saga of the Muses

"Here comes Dick, See Dick run.
Run Dick run.
Here comes Jane, See Jane run, run Jane run.
See Spot Jump, Jump Spot Jump.
See Baby go, Go Baby go."

Needless to say, by the time all the students in the class had read, we didn't care whether Dick ran, Jane jumped or Spot had eaten the baby. (But however silly the book was, it must have worked, for most of us never forgot that little book on which we cut our first literary teeth.)

By then the only thing that mattered to us was "Recess Time," when we would all go outside to play rubber or soft ball for an hour or so, around mid-day. Those of us who were not interested in playing ball would find other games to play, like "Little Sally Walker"; "Hide and Seek"; "Dropping the Handkerchief"; Or many times we would find ourselves vigorously doing the "Jitterbug," under the unusually high area beneath the church, which was cut out and built up to form the raised plat-form inside the sanctuary; and was made even higher by the constant erosion caused by rushing rainwater washing away the dirt that skirted the rapidly decaying building above us.

As you can see, we kids lived for this play period, and we planned our activities from one to two days ahead. We were also very choosy as to whom our team mates were and we would often bargain with our favorites, by sharing our pocket change or lunch with them far in advance of the day of the teams performance. When the recess period was over we would drag ourselves back into the classroom, too exhausted to read or do the required school work for the rest of the day, only to repeat this process from day to day, five days each week, Mondays through Fridays.

22

Chapter 5

The Day I Prayed for Mama Lillie's Death

Let there be no mistake as to how we loved Mama Lillie. Despite the fact that she was a very strong and consistent disciplinarian, she was still the object of our affection, as far as our love for parents were concern. And we often expressed among ourselves that if we had choice as to which parent would die first, we would cast our vote against our mothers, in favor of keeping Mama Lillie alive and with us. That being the case, you may wonder just how then could you possibly have been tempted to pray for her death? Well, it is a long story, but it is as follows:

Around my third year in school, the old school building that was already leaning and reeking with age had deteriorated to an unsafe and threatening condition. Therefore, the local PTA organization along with members of the community, decided to launch a building program to build a new schoolhouse to replace the existing one.

Every one was responsible for raising as much money as possible, and or buy so many feet of lumber, or nails, bricks or other such items as were needed in the building

23

of the new school house. Students too, were given coin envelopes (which we called "Begging Envelopes") to aid in this very worthwhile project. Well, even though I was the teacher's pet and her little "One Hundred boy." My fund raising was not going too well, and my infantile pride would not bear me to be beaten by any other student, at least, none of those in my class. Although I had gotten a number of promises from other members of the family and other adults from time to time, things just weren't working out for me in this effort.

The big moment came in a form of temptation, which allowed me to increase my grand total of thirty cents by four more cents, thus giving me a total of thirty-four cents. Which indeed was a lot of money to me, and I was sure that it would go quite far toward the building of the new schoolhouse. It all happened one morning as I passed by our rural mail box with its door flap partly opened, its flag raised, and inside I saw a letter with four pennies on it, three of which were for postage for the letter, and one was for a post card. (This was the usual way that most mail was sent in the country at that time.) Tempted, I took the pennies and placed them in my envelope, and I carried the letter home to Mama Lillie, telling her that I had seen the mailman open the box, and take the pennies but not the letter. I was even dumb enough to, with the next breath; tell her that I had been given four pennies for my envelope by an old man whom we called "Mr. Big Dad," as he was cutting tall grass from the ditch banks and piling it in the bottom of the ditch on which he steadily worked about a mile from the house.

It was quite apparent that Mama Lillie didn't buy my story, for she ordered me not to go to school until she got back,

24

then she hurried off to find Mr. Big Dad, whereupon, finding him, he informed her that he had not seen me all morning. Of course, he had seen me that morning but he had not given me the pennies as I had claimed. Mama Lillie had gotten to the bottom of my falsehood, and that was very bad for me, as I saw her on her way back to the house where I was waiting all alone for her return. The other children had already left me knowing full well just what I could expect when she returned.

I anxiously watched through tear-blinded eyes, as Mama Lillie neared the house, I watched her as she carefully tucked her apron under her belt. (She always wore an apron, which had been a sort of trademark of hers as long as I could remember. It always adorned her longer- than- usual dress, which was always sparkling clean no matter how hard she worked around the house.) Now she tucks it under her belt. She then spat in her hand, and rubbing them together, as if to torture my fearful soul even more than it already was. She steps into the wayside woods that skirted a dip in the road that often flooded when it rained, which we called the "Little Pond". She then breaks a small tree, not a limb or branch, but a tree.

She again preceded toward the house stripping the leaves away, as she slowly tortures me with her dreadful approach. I wanted to hide, but there was no place to hide where she couldn't find me. I wanted to run, but there was no place to go. I therefore stood crying and praying. "Lord please kill Mama Lillie, for if you don't, I know that she is going to kill me." Of course, I wouldn't be so lucky. My "Day of Doom" had come, and Mama Lillie would serve as judge, jury and executioner, all in one. There was no possible appeal. And I was not even spared the time or mercy to properly plan for disposal of the remains. Nor was

I sure that there would be enough left to dispose of when it was all over any way.

Mama Lillie pounced upon me with the fury of an angry wild cat, swinging her tree with perfect accuracy and out preaching a Baptist preacher as she lectured to me about stealing and lying about it, which to her, next to killing someone, was the worst of all crimes. She chased and whipped me around the house for, what seemed to me an eternity. The many limbs on the tree made for five or more whipping in one, as each one left its telling mark some where on my quivering frame. Their biting pain was only exceeded by my loud uncontrollable cry and sincere plea for mercy from my angry great grandmother. And to make matters worse, she had the unmitigated gall to claim that she was whipping me because she loved me. Boy, I found that hard to believe that morning.

Finally, there was a break in her lecture, but not in her whipping, as she ordered me to pick up my books and "get to school". Of course, by then I was happy just to go to school, even without the books just to get away from her. I anxiously grabbed my books and running as fast as I could toward the pond for school. But as fast as I ran, I could not out-run her nor escape the fierce lashes of her tree- wielding swinging right hand, as she fiercely chased me into the pond whipping me all along the way.

As we entered the pond, I was sort of counting on the bull frogs which always sang day and night in the water and tall grasses of that pond, to save me from her ever pursuing wrath. — You see, Mama Lillie was awfully fearful of frogs, all frogs, little ones, big ones, it didn't matter, if it was a frog, she was afraid of it. —And I knew that once she heard one frog croak, she would panic and turn around and hurry back home, leaving me to dry my tears and compose myself before I got to the school. But was I in for a shocking surprise, as the only voice heard in that pond that morning was mine. Not a single frog uttered even the smallest squeak. And the way Mama Lillie was beating on me, she deserved a good scare, I thought. She finally turned around and made her way back through the pond, and, what do you know? Almost as if some unseen director directed them; the frogs burst into their usual singing. Only this time, they seemed louder than ever before. Therefore, when ever I hear the croaking of frogs, even to this day, I am reminded of the worst whipping of my life, and all because of a few lousy pennies that I collected in good faith, to raise money to help build a school house. And mind you, I am glad that Mama Lillie didn't die as I prayed that she would. And neither did I die at her hands. Further more, I was made a more honest person because of it all, for I was cured of petty thievery from that day on.

By the time I got to school that day I had recovered enough to assume my usual place at the head of my class. Apart from a few bruises and welts, the only damage having been done was to my pride, as all the children (at least those from our house) knew that I had just gotten the whipping of my life. They seemed to stare at me wondering just how I had managed to survive the gruesome ordeal. I was convinced that while some of them felt sorry for me. others, though they dared not say, were happy about it. Never the less, I made it, and with that I vowed that I would never steal again, nor ever again use those cursed coin envelopes, not even for legitimate purposes like giving my offering at church, I simply write a check instead.

(Furthermore, as it would turn out, for the rest of my life just about all my future earnings would be spent in either the up- building of schools or toward the operation of some school, somewhere. Not to mention the many years that I would spend teaching at schools that couldn't afford to pay even the smallest of salary. The greatest of all sacrifice would come in time, as I would found the Montgomery Bible Institute and Theological Center which would consume just about all that I can beg, borrow or scrape, as so to speak.)

In time, our family grew with the birth of our oldest sister Lucile (Mae) in 1940, and the next older sister, Mary Pearl, in 1942, who was born before Mama Lillie's death in 1946. Lucile, barely remembering her, mainly by her sheer disciplinarian practices. While Pearl, was too young to remember anything at all about her. Another sister, Minnie, would be born in 1948. A brother named Joe Louis, in 1949, followed her birth. Another sister, Ida Bell would follow in 1951. Another brother Richard would come along in 1953. And finally our baby brother, Jimmy would come along in 1954.Thereby completing the Muse clan, which remained in tact and a close knitted family even after they all married and had children of their own.

The Day That Mama Lillie Died

As time went on, we all watched with great concern, as Mama Lillie became more and more feeble. Headaches became more frequently and the ever-present camphor odor was evident of her secret usage of it during the night before we arose and got started in the mornings. Those of us who were around her most often, heard her groan a bit more as she gently rubbed her head throughout the day.

Never the less, despite her obvious pain, she seemed to have been more concern in leaving fond memories of herself with the family. For instance, instead of her usual contentment with the magazine and newspaper covered walls in her room, she had her walls plastered with new wallpaper, and hang long sheer curtains at the two windows with solid panels that matched the pattern on the new linoleum. These panels hung on both sides of the sheer curtains that hang loosely over the windows that were cut through the wall on two sides of the room, and always swayed as the wind briskly moved them as it blew through the pane- less open windows, which were open during the day for light and swing close by night for security.

Instead of the throw rugs that she always used on the bare floor, she went out and bought an expensive blue and floral design linoleum, the first that I can ever remember seeing or noticing. She seems to have been literally setting her house in order. She also bought new furniture, including oversized stuffed chairs and a day bed, which served as a sofa during the day, and doubled as a pullout bed at night. Little did we expect that her remaining time with us would be so short and come so soon.

We also noticed that she became less preoccupied with disciplining the children, choosing rather to speak a bit kinder and gentler to us instead. After all, we were becoming of age by then, and I guess that she was observing the effect that her earlier years of discipline had on our lives. By this time Baby Sister and I had become eleven years of age, and both of us noticed a curious air of expectancy that seemed so prevalent throughout the house. There was a feeling that something was about to happen, and yet we knew not what. We even talked about what a great loss we would suffer if Mama Lillie were to die. We seemed to have had a premonition from signs that always jumped out at us from every quarter of the house, which somehow intensified our feeling that something was indeed about to happen.

Then, on a cold, dreary and foggy February morning, our worst fear began to unfold into a living reality. My mother and her sister Mary stood anxiously beside the bed whereon Mama Lillie lay. They took terms in rubbing her head with a loud smelling camphor mixture. We could not but notice the seriousness of their concern, as they summon one of the boys to run to the "Big House" and have them to call the doctor. Through all this, Mama Lillie lay without saying a word; only continuous groans came from her mouth. And then, she seemed to have stopped breathing for a spell, which intensified the panic, which the women had experienced throughout the morning hours. Sharp wails from them sent shock waves through the hearts of the children as they heard their screams. And just then, true to the nature of Mama Lillie, she awoke for a brief spell, and begins talking in a calm voice to the women that stood over her bed.

Like the Old Testament character (Jacob) who prophesied and blessed his children, one-by-one, leaning upon his staff. So too, Mama Lillie lying on her deathbed did the same for her grand children. One by one, and name-by-name, she cautioned our mothers about their children. She especially cautioned our aunt Mary to give special attention to her son "Man" who seemed to have been viewed as a somewhat problem child by her even back then. She urged them to use patience and understanding with some of us, assuring them that none of us were really bad children.

By then the news that the doctor was near had reached the room. As he had to park his car on the dry side of the

30

"Little Pond" and putting on his rubber boots, he walked up to the house and went immediately to Mama Lillie's bedside. Whereupon after a brief examination, he concluded that she had had a very serious stroke and that her chance for survival was very slim. He then proceeded to give her a shot in the arm, and to everyone's surprise, Mama Lillie didn't object at all. For it was a known fact that Mama Lillie had only two great fears in her life, one was frogs and the other were shot needles. In the past when the doctor attempted to give her a shot she would panic out of fear of the needle, begging anyone near "Please don't let him give me a shot." And knowing that she would have had to be held down or tied up to be given the shot, the doctor always opted to give her medicine instead. But on this morning she never showed any concern when he mentioned a shot, neither did she even flinch when he pressed the needle into her arm.

Having completed his task, the doctor once again reminded the family of the severity of the stroke and that we may not expect Mama Lillie to be with us very long because of it. He walks back to his parked car on the other side of the pond, and in a flash, he was gone. He had barely gotten out of sight, when Mama Lillie slumped her head on her pillow, and just like that! The grand old lady, who was the inspiration of so many lives, was gone. Mama Lillie was dead leaving a gaping void in our hearts that have yet to be filled even after all these years. She was buried a few days later. Her funeral was held at the church that sat in front of the schoolhouse. Hers was more traditional and far less dramatic than Pa Daddy's was. There was a hearse, a church funeral, and all the extras that go along with a modern day Christian funeral. There's no need for an extended elaboration on her funeral in this account since nothing out of the ordinary took place during this celebration. But needless to say, Mama Lillie's influence has impacted our lives more than any single person on this earth ever could.

Well. The new school was finally built, which was a far cut above the old one. Instead of a single room building, there were two rooms. Where in the old building the panes were broken in the windows, in the new school there were larger and brighter windows. There was an outside porch in the middle of the building that led into a hall that divided the classrooms. Instead of one teacher, there were two new teachers. And with the added grades we could go through the sixth grade before having to leave for another school.

With my old teacher having gone, regretful to say, I lost my "One Hundred Boy" status. And my new homeroom teacher was rather brutish and unkind to most of the students, but especially to those of us from Mr. X's plantation. It appeared that instead of her seeking our strengths, she was more interested in proving that we were ignorant and unteachable. Never the less, I studied hard and with this and such teaching as she did, I was able to pass the required tests that enabled me to pass from the sixth grade and transfer to another school where I would remain until my graduation from high school.

Boy, do I remember all too well the day of the test. We were drilled for the greater part of the year in intensive study of major subjects required by the public school system, in order to be promoted from the sixth to the seventh grade. We were gathered at the Dallas County Training School in Beloit, for the exam. In my estimation there were about three to five hundred students taking the test there that day. All day we worked until early evening. And we were to reassemble the next week at the Brown Chapel church in Selma, to get the results.

When the time came for us to go to Selma, I was so worried and excited that I couldn't eat breakfast. We were taken to the church and the roll call began of students having passed the exam. Of course I was sweating bullets, so to speak, thinking that somehow I may have flunked the exam, especially after some two or three hundred names were called. And what a relief it was to me, when I was just about to die of panic, they called my name: WILLIE LEE MUSE, I flew like a bat out of Montgomery and took my place among the winners, rejoicing forever more.

The first two years after Mama Lillie's death, most of the children desiring to one day join her and be with her in heaven, joined the church and were baptized on the first Sunday in August of that year. I of course, was a bit less believing, and would not join until the second year. I accepted Christ on Thursday night of our annual revival services and I too, was baptized in August of that second year.

The pool was located outside behind the church, and had waist-high cement walls and steps on both outside and inside of it. Because there was no plumbing, the pool was filled with water that was hauled in barrels by tractor or mule drawn trailer from a creek several miles away, which took the better part of several days to fill. And as always, there were large numbers of candidates baptized that year as were each year, and yet the church never seemed to get any larger. Mr. X and his family often came to the baptisms. He would pull his car right up near the pool and they would sit in it throughout the service. Until, one day the pastor, fed up with this action, publicly ask him to back his car away so that worshippers could get near the pool. After which they never again came to our baptism services. Even though they understood that they were always welcome to stand or sit with other worshippers no matter the occasion.

Chapter 6

Life on the Plantation

Having reached school age, little did I realize that I had also reached the age that made me, as a "share cropper's child", to begin working in the cotton fields. At first I was given the task of "water boy" which made me responsible to take water to the field hands so that they would not have to stop their chopping the cotton or corn to walk to, the sometime far away pump to quince their thirst. At first, I was the water boy for my family members as they worked the large field with seemingly endless rows that was allotted to them to work. Then there were those rare occasions when I had the task to take water to a larger company of workers as they all worked in certain fields together. I would carry the water in a large tin bucket that was much too heavy to carry full, from the often far away pump, down long freshly plowed cotton rows, straining and splashing as I go, with bucket in one hand and a drinking dipper or gourd in the other. I would move from person to person as they drank from a common dipper. Having given them all a drink, I repeated this process in unbroken continuity throughout the long hot and sultry summer days. Such was the case whether it was the planting, growing or harvest season. During the harvest season I would have to hold the bucket high over-head to avoid getting it full of cotton leaves or other debris falling from the tall stalks of cotton. This was indeed an awesome task for any seven or eight year old, but especially for me since I was rather frail and a bit lazy, if I may so admit. And fieldwork was not my favorite pass-time.

Furthermore, this field work always kept us out of school both during the planting, growing, and harvest seasons, which always caused us to lag behind other students attending our school, most of whom were able to begin when school first opened and remain throughout the year. However, having come of age, I would be responsible to carry my own row in the hoeing and the picking of cotton, which usually was from sunup to sunset, five and a half days each week, unless we were blessed with an early morning or midday rain, which was always received with much glee and thanksgiving, for to us, this meant that we could go to school at least one day more during that season, only to return to the field as soon as it was dry enough to resume the working or the gathering of the crops.

Of course, these unneeded rains never set well with the boss man, (whom throughout the rest of this narrative will be referred to as "Mr. X" or simply the "Boss Man".) For on rainy days his voice could always be heard cursing with the fervor of a holiness preacher or a cackling sage hen. He would sing in unbroken continuity, "God d..; God d..; God d..; God d..;" He would even sometime add a loud shriek. He usually ended this statement with a loud shout, as if he was possessed with some kind of controlling spirit that compelled him to act that way. One day he added. "I wish the damn lightening would strike me down right now." Of course, most of us silently cast our vote in favor of the same, while at the same time allowing enough space between him and us so that we would not get electrocuted during the process nor become spattered with his bloody evil remains.

There are perhaps, those who may raise the question as to whether the farm on which we lived fit the description of a "plantation." Let me present the facts as we experienced, that you may make your own decision about it. And I am certain that you will at least conclude that it was a "shadow plantation." Since living and working conditions were just as hard and verbal and sometimes even physical abuses were just as harsh- at least for some. For like the Japanese soldier who kept hiding and fighting in the jungle for many years, unaware that the war had ended years earlier. So too, Mr. X, seemed to have been unaware that Lincoln had long since freed the slaves in this country. He therefore inflicted the many share- cropper families who lived on his land with similar slave-like conditions through out the years during that time.

Unless there was a high status crime committed on the plantation, such as murder or in some cases, grand larceny, Mr. X served as sheriff, judge and jury himself for persons committing such crime who were living on his plantation. He often boasted that he could get them out of anything that they got into except hell. I even witnessed one case when he hit one young man in the eye leaving a gaping gash and a black eye for hiding in the local movie house and robbing its safe after it was closed. This young man told us later that Mr. X's wife held the pistol on him while Mr. X brutalized him. However, when there was a murder committed, (I can recall one such case) he was forced to call the sheriff to make the arrest. Otherwise, no lawman ever set foot on his place unless he was going on one of the frequent dove hunts with him or some other unofficial event that he was hosting. Incidentally, I can't recall any one from his plantation ever being drafted into the army or any other form of military service, even though a very devastating world war was raging and things weren't going very well for our nation and its allies. These things only added to his pride as to what a powerful and influential man he was.

The people were literally bound to the land, tied by cords of indebtedness and always lacking "that one bale of cotton" to pay their debt for money that they were advanced to buy food, clothing and other necessities for themselves or their families during the year. Therefore, no one hardly ever left the plantation to live elsewhere unless they ran away unknown to Mr. X. Once away, they were afraid to come back, even to visit loved ones or to attend funerals of family members or friends. Hard times and bad luck sometimes would cause some of them to ignore their fears and return to the plantation. Others never returned no matter how tough life became for them.

Our family, on the other hand, was always treated with a certain noticed level of respect, maybe because of the economical value because of its size. Or maybe because of the way our mother cared for her household, and therefore, neither Mr. X nor any other person desired to entangle with her in the defense of her children. Although she was a small and quiet woman, once she became angry, she was as mean as a scalded rattlesnake and twice as deadly. On one occasion a little "straw boss" threatened my brother, and she immediately confronted him telling him that only she was expected to discipline her children. And that nobody else had better ever touch any one of them. I think that he got the message.

Mr. X also showed respect and partiality toward our family in several ways. For instance once the crop was up enough for him to turn it over to our family, he never came among us in the field giving instruction or criticizing the work that was being done. While in some other families he was always there making sure that the work was being done according to his liking. He also gave special consideration to me, as I would often go to him to borrow money for school supplies and other necessities. He would often single me out of a long line of other men of the farm who were seeking advancement in pay in order to buy things for themselves or their family. Screaming in a loud voice, he would say to them, "Y'all act like you think that I am made of money, I don't have any." Getting the drop on them, he would say to me, "Preacher, (the nick name that he gave me) what do you want?" I told him that I needed some money. He said, "Preacher, come back after these other boys (who were actually men) are gone. You know that I am going to help you." He once even said to me; "As long as you don't run around all times of night, drinking that old bad whiskey, and running around with all those old bad women like these other boys, you can count on my help in anything you attempt to do." More than a few times this was his response to my request when I went to him seeking assistance. He even called me into his office one day and in the presence of his wife, he repeated the same. He assured me that even if he was not there, that she would help me the same as he would. She nodded her head in agreement.

The Saga of the Muses

Mr. X's interest in me may have been because of a special dreamed-up project of mine very early in my teen years. You see, I was always interested in airplanes, many of which always flew over the fields and buzzed our homes as they practiced their war-time maneuvers before returning to Craig Air force base some fifteen or twenty miles away. Pilots were being prepared for combat mission, as World War II, was raging in many parts of the world at that time. Watching them fly their planes overhead each day simply fascinated me.

However, my interest in planes became most irresistible one day when I had the opportunity to observe a crop-dusting plane close-up, as they were refilling it on a makeshift landing strip in an oat field not very far from our house. I just couldn't take it any longer. I decided that I would build myself an "almost" full size plane out of sweet gum poles and fertilizer bags. I put three wheelbarrow wheels on it. I then cut a large windmill and attached it to the front of the plane, giving it the appearance that its motor was running when the wind blew on it as it sat under a large pine tree not very far from our house, when we were not pushing someone in it along the dusty road that led to the house.

Mr. X brought his friends and family members by to see it time and time again, leaving them scratching their heads in amazement as he laughingly told them "Preacher made that damn thing out of sweet-gum poles and soda bags." It also fooled the pilot of the crop duster plane, for he asked, "Whose plane was idling under that tree?" After that time Mr. X suggested that he would send me to trade school to be a mechanic so that I would come back and repair his tractors and other farm machinery. Of course, he reminded me of his on-going expectation when I informed him that I was leaving the farm several years later.

In the meanwhile, life for me on the plantation was very hard and trying. As you may remember from an earlier chapter, our house was completely without electricity or other utilities such as gas or oil burning stove or heaters. Therefore, all heating, cooking, ironing and heating of water, was done by wood burning fires. (Of course, this would pose a major challenge for me in later years, being the oldest child, and having to cut and haul the wood for these fires, mostly without help from any one. And sometimes, I even had to carry it on my shoulder from the nearby woods to the house.) This of course, left one of my shoulders slightly lower than the other, which to me is a badge of love to my dear mother and family that meant the entire world to me.

However, most times I would venture into the distant woods with my sharp single blade axe, searching until I located enough trees as close together as possible, to make a wagon load. I would then furiously chop down large and small trees and then chop them into wagon length. Having done so, I then would go and borrow mules and a wagon from the "big barn." After loading the heavy logs all by myself, I would proudly, but exhaustingly parade slowly along the dirt roads toward home, leaving the boss man and field hands that I encountered along the way, alike, amazed and puzzled that I had loaded such big logs all by myself, being the frail young man that I was. (It was during one of these wood cutting ventures that I dropped the sharp axe on the ball of my right foot, and sustained an injury that required several stitches, that would prevent me from qualifying for the basketball team during my senior year of high school.)

41

Once again, I became "water boy" this time for the team, in order that I might travel with them when they played games away from home.

Once home, the wood was unloaded on the wood pile which would become my daily work place as I chopped firewood to keep the family warm and fed during the long wintry days and nights. Although the work was hard and very laborious, I did it most joyfully for my mother and family whom I felt deserved all that I could do for them and much more.

Never the less, I still found myself longing for the day when I would grow up and move them from this very oppressive situation, an opportunity that would not come until one and a half years after I had finished high school. This account will be given in dramatic details in a chapter especially designated for this important event.

Life during My High School Years

Life on the farm was never easy especially during the work season. And it was just as hard and most challenging during my high school years. We were always late getting into school during the fall due to our involvement in the harvesting of the crop. In the spring, the planting season always made us late. However, once in, we were thrusted into an entirely new world with problems and challenges that were unique and unknown to us back on the plantation. For instance, there were the problems of peer pressure among fellow students and the obvious lack of preference by certain teachers who seemed to sort of resent us because we were from the plantation, and maybe because we delayed the class by our late entrance.

Furthermore, we had to brave the weather be it hot and dry or cold and rainy. There were no busses to carry us to school. When bus service eventually became available, it was decided that we lived too close to the school to be afforded the service. We therefore had to walk a distance that seemed to have been too far for any student to walk, especially on cold wintry days, and often in the rain. (However, upon returning home after many years and driving that route, I couldn't believe just how close we actually lived to it, after checking the distance on the car's speedometer. I concluded that this was the longest mile that anyone ever had to walk, it somehow seemed to have diminished with time.)

However we were determined to make the very best of our time while there despite those unfavorable circumstances. This determination compelled me to become innovative during my junior year in high school. While most young men, at lease those from the plantation and surrounding farms, were compelled to wear brogan (high top) work shoes to school. For most of us had only two pairs of shoes, one pair for Sunday dress only, and the other were course every-day work shoes, which some of us, were to wear to school instead of those that we used for dress. Well, at least two young men from one family declared, that before they would wear those shoes to school, they would drop out all together. They concluded by doing just that before completing their junior year. I, on the other hand, decided that I would somehow, change the image of my having to wear those shoes. I therefore polished and shined mine and bought a pair of wide plaid strings for them. I then stiffly starched my dungarees (blue jeans) using cooking flour for starch, and ironing them with a single fold, three or four inch cuff that hung high above the shoe top. I therefore, feel that I had created a "fad" as I noticed during the next few weeks just about all the young men at our school - even those who were not compelled to do so- were sporting these changes in their dress. This style seemed to spread like wild fire, even to other schools in and near the area.

(Many years later, I would have the privilege of teaching one of those young men that dropped out, while I taught at Selma University, "a small Baptist college noted for training of ministers at Selma, Alabama" as he had passed the G.E.D test after he had received his call to preach the Gospel. Obviously his pride had set him back many years and cost him many precious opportunities of service in the Christian ministry.)

Meanwhile, after initiating the fad, I became accepted among the more popular young men at the school, as I was perceived somewhat of a model among them, and it certainly didn't hurt my relationship with the young ladies in the mean time. I was able to move freely and easily among them and in the classroom I was simply invincible. I took most teachers challenge at learning and usually came out at the head of the class. That is any class except Math, which was my worse subject even while I attended college several years later.

As my graduation year was rapidly approaching my mother, having some concern with my father's promise to help with the expenses of graduation. He had promised to buy my class ring, a new suit of clothes and pay such fees as were associated with that long-awaited-day. He seldom if ever, kept his promises to me during my growing-up years. She therefore, in the attempt to ward off such disappointment, gave me a pig and a calf a year earlier, to raise and sell for this purpose. Boy, you can't imagine the amount of love and care that I heaped upon these animals. Day after day I gathered corn and pulp weeds for the pig, always making sure that he had plenty of clean water to drink, along with extra water for him to wallow in to keep himself cool during the hot summer days. Such care and pampering turned him into a fat and fine pig.

Similar attention was given to the calf. I literally nursed that calf and gave him the care that calves never got, at least, not on that plantation. Someone gave me an old curl comb, (a comb used to groom show horses on the farm) with which I groomed and brushed the calf's hair day after day. I constantly gathered tall Johnson grass for hay in order that he may have food enough so that he would never go hungry, or have to sleep on the bare ground only if he chose to so. Such fine care turned him into a gentle, fat and fine calf. I therefore, with mixed emotions looked to the day that I would have to sell him for the purpose for which he was given to me in the first place. But as luck would have it that dreaded day would never come. For about a month before I was to sell him, the calf took sick over night and died that same night. Needless to say, the death of that calf was the most devastating disappointment that I had ever known. It was almost like losing a close friend or relative. This grief coupled with the fact that I still needed the money that selling him would have brought, was almost more than I could bear. My world simply crumbled for I had worked so hard and looked so long for graduation. And now all my hope was dashed to smithereens overnight. Some young men around me didn't offer much help by cruelly joking me saying, "Preacher, (the nick name that I had come to accept) the buzzards are eating your suit and class ring. What are you going to do now?" Not knowing what to say to them. I simply faked a smile and told them they were correct, without further comment in an effort to hold back the tears that were rapidly swelling in my eyes. For in my infantile pride, as a man, I was not supposed to cry nor ever display any signs of weakness if I was to maintain my guarded social status among my peers.

Once again Mr. X came to the rescue. Several days later seeing him about the farm, he said to me "Preacher, I was told that your calf died. That was a very fine calf; I was looking forward to buying it from you. Had you informed me that he was sick I would have had the veterinarian to look at him." I told him that I didn't know that he was sick. He continued. "I understand that you were raising him to sell to take care of your graduation expenses." I answered in the affirmative. He said "Preacher, I will make you a deal, if you would sell me your pig, I will give you as much for him as I would have given you for both the calf and the pig had you sold them to me. In other words, I will more than double what the pig is worth." Of course this deal was struck and it greatly lifted an insurmountable burden for me so far as graduation expenses were concerned. And like my mother had thought, we never heard a word from my dad.

Graduation day came several weeks later, and I marched across the stage wearing a brand new suit with all new accessories that went along with it, a gold class ring on my finger, and I didn't owe anyone one dime as I proudly received my diploma, missing the top honor of valedictorian, only because I was not the principal's daughter. I was therefore, resigned to accept the second highest of salutatorian. For me it didn't matter that someone deliberately hid or misplaced my transcript, only having it to reappear several years later as I was attempting to enroll in college. Honor or not, I made it through, and was the first male from the plantation to have ever done so, which was only preceded by one female, "Gracie Mae", who graduated a year earlier.

After graduation, I worked the rest of that year until the harvest was over. I worked in the field driving the tractor during the day and sometimes even during the night with the aid of special lights rigged on it for that purpose. I also was involved in picking and weighing the cotton, when Mr. X had to be away on business or attending a horse show that was too far for his timely return. All the time I was busily preparing to leave the farm by the end of October. As the time of my departure drew near I began to think and reflect on some of the things and people that I would be leaving behind when I left for the city.

Chapter 7

Reflections on people and things being left behind

With preparation being made for my departure, I found time to reflect on people and other things that I would be leaving behind. In addition to other family members I regretted most of all about having to leave a precious little baby daughter "Mary Ann" who was born during my junior year in high school. Her mother concluded that for us to have married would terribly disrupt my plans and we should therefore not do so but wait for a later time to see how things would work out. Well needless to say, things didn't work out too well for us as she married an archrival of mine and moved to Mobile a year later.

Mary Ann embodied all of the characteristics of people that were endeared to me. She was as beautiful and kind as her mother whom I truly adored. She inherited the complexion and persona of Mama Lillie. And the quiet and easy going nature, spirit and voice of my mother, so much so that when I call her today, many years after mothers death, when she answers the phone, she sounds every bit like her, even using the greeting phrase that was so uniquely mother's way of greeting me. "Hey Rev." She also inherited some of my childhood physical weaknesses and frailties, which resulted in her having to be hospitalized quite often during her growing-up years. Despite it all, she grew up to be a very fine and beautiful young lady, and the mother of two wonderful sons, Cedric and Eugene.

"Baby Sister" had already married and started a family; therefore she would no longer be living with the family, as she had done practically all of our lives. I therefore wondered just what it would be like without her living with the rest of the family, and being looked after by my mother who had raised us together since she was a very small girl. Although she was my aunt on mother's side of the family and my first cousin on father's side, most people thought of us as brother and sister. (Her very best friend Gracie Mae, who was a close friend to both of us, had already left the plantation to live in Detroit, where she would remain until her death in the late 90's.)

Also, I could not help but thinking about "Old Blackie" the wolf-looking black dog whose coat was jet black mingled with a curly gray. He was a bit larger than the other dogs around the house; "Old She Wee, and "White Gal." In fact, he was larger than any dogs on the plantation. He was a stray that took up at our house during my high school years, and although he was rather clumsy at times, he was fast and gentle. But most of all, Old Blackie was my friend. Even though most times I wouldn't see him nor know where he was. I only had to do a certain whistle and Old Blackie could be heard racing through the cotton or corn field, where he may have been wandering in search for rabbits or other small game, ending up panting at my side no matter whether it was rain or shine, night or day. So far as I can remember, he never once failed to respond to my summoning whistle.

On nights when I would go a- courting, it was always very assuring to have Old Blackie accompanying me through the back-roads and across the fields to my girlfriend's house some two or three miles away. (I always walked, as I didn't have a bike or car as some of the fellows did). Old Blackie would chase rabbits along the road side or the woods edge all along the way, never straying too long before he was at my side again. Once at the house, he would sleep or rest on the porch until I left the house only to repeat the same process on our way back home. Now that I was about to leave, there seemed to have been a note of sadness on his face as if he was aware of just what was about to happen, a sadness that matched that which I felt in my heart as I knew that I was about to leave him. For as fate would have it, once I left, I would never see Old Blackie again. I don't know whether he just wandered away to find another home, just as he had first wandered to our house, or whether he just went away and died of a broken heart.

Then there were two old very dark Black men, Mr. Tangy and his twin brother, Scorefield. They were very unique in that they were old and not at all handsome, and neither would win a beauty contest even if he were the only contestant. Besides, they both had a peg leg and each drove a two-wheel ox cart wherever they went. Sometimes they would ride in the same cart, but occasionally they would trail one behind the other each in his own wagon. They crept along the gravel road at a snail's pace, which seemed to take them forever to pass through the plantation once they were seen approaching in the far distant. The ox that pulled the cart would barely move one foot ahead the other as they crept along the way, until they would finally fade into the horizon down the long dusty road until they vanished into the miles. We kids called them "rain-hawks" because it seemed to have always rained shortly after they passed through the farm.

The rumor as to how they both being twins came to have a peg leg each was very strange. It is said that one of them was far from home and was attempting to hobo a train back home when he slipped beneath the train and lost his leg. The other one upon hearing of this tragedy, attempted to hobo a train to go to him when he too, slipped beneath the train and lost a leg. One lost his right leg and the other his left. Therefore since they wore the same size shoe, it is said that they would alternate in buying a pair of shoes and each would share his with the other. The one thing that they didn't share however, were their "colt forty five" pistols which each carried hidden somewhere in or near his peg leg which allowed them to out-draw anyone in the surrounding area so far as fire arms were involved. Local lawmen never forbade their carrying weapons since they were both considered handicapped. Rumors have it, that they were always a bit tipsy whenever they crept along the roadway, a condition which did absolutely nothing to enhance their ruddy and down-home appearance.

Then, there was my unforgettable cousin "Man", who was the perfect personification of the storybook character, "Bad, Bad, Leroy Brown" of the plantation. Man, too, loved his "stump juice". But whether he was juiced up or not, he would crash every party within a ten mile radius, on and off the plantation, confronting just about everyone he met challenging them to the fight of their life. Most people would shutter at the news that "Man Mule" (as he was called) had arrived at the party. Some would make an early exit leaving the party before time so they would not have to confront him. I too have left a few parties upon learning that he was there. There is no end to the disastrous problems that he has encountered at these parties and other places, which he would go week after week over the years. For instance, at one such party an uncle of mine firing a pistol, shot him in the leg, and carried him home and put him in bed.

Another time he was hit in the head with a two-by-four, leaving a permanent dent in his skull. Several times he sustained injuries when he was stabbed or cut while attending different parties or in scuffles elsewhere in the area. He has totally wrecked more cars and trucks that I am able to remember, and through all he sustained very minor, or in most cases, no injury at all. But the real duzzie came one Sunday as he was riding a horse, which he had borrowed from the "big barn." After having had too much to drink, he was racing the horse as fast as the poor creature could run, when suddenly the horse fell and broke both front legs. Of course, it had to be destroyed, but Man was so inebriated that he didn't know just what had happened until the next day after the affect his booze had worn off. This leaving me to think that he has more lives than a nine-life cat.

Many years later I saw Mr. X at a school-political function, (as he had become a County Commissioner,) and he jokingly said to me, "Preacher, your cousin Man doesn't believe that drinking whiskey will kill him, even though the doctor has told him that if he takes one more drink he will surely die." I told him neither did I think that it will kill him, for if it will he would have already died. He laughed out loud and said, "You know you just may be right." Well as time would have it, since then both the doctor and Mr. X have died, and as of today, (the time of this writing) Man is still alive and is still drinking as always. However, I don't think that he is as active in those other areas that I previously mentioned because of his age and his level of maturity during these late days. This is another sign of one of those more than a nine-life cat life he has that I mentioned earlier in reference to him.

How could I ever forget my very best friend and running buddy, Edward, whom we called "Bubba"? Bubba and I were all but inseparable, for whenever you saw one of us you would always see the other. In fact, most people referred to us as each other's shadow. Between us we pledged that if either had a nickel the other could claim two and a half cents of the same. In spite of it all, I was leaving Bubba behind. (He of course would leave the farm sometime later to life in Chicago, where he would remain until his death in the mid 90's) which left a gaping hole in my memories of growing-up on the plantation. I have many fond and cherished memories of many pleasant and unforgettable times that we spent together as friends and brothers beloved during those very difficult and trying years of growing up on the farm.

Lastly, in a somewhat appreciative but childish way, I could not help but think of "Old Mat" and "Old Beauty" the family cows, who were sort of a lifeline for us, as without their warm milk, many days we would not have had anything for breakfast before we left for the field or school. Often we had to beat their calves to them for the first to get to them get the milk for that morning. Old Mat also gave birth to the calf that I raised to sell to pay my graduation expenses. Even though they were only dumb farm animals, somehow they seemed even closer than many of our friends or family members to us.

These were few but fond and lasting memories that were mine that brought on mixed emotions as I prepared to leave the plantation to take up living in Montgomery, with a never-to-be-realized plan to continue on to Omaha, Nebraska a few months later, where I had planned to live with my father's sister Leola, after I would have bought sufficient clothes to withstand the very harsh winters there. Little did I know that I would be in Montgomery for the rest of my life, barring some un-for-see-able and unsettling circumstances.

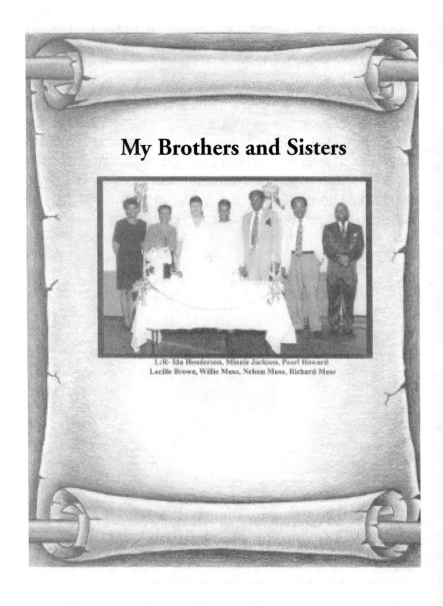

My Brothers and Sisters

L:R- Ida Henderson, Minnie Jackson, Pearl Howard
Lucille Brown, Willie Muse, Nelson Muse, Richard Muse

My Brothers and Sisters

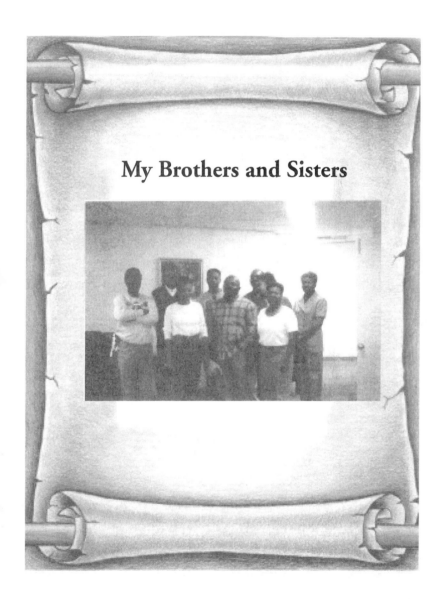

Chapter 8

Leaving the Plantation for Life in the City
(Autumn 1954 - Spring 1956)

Having completed the harvest, I anxiously, but with much hesitation, awaited my father to come for me and take me to Montgomery, where I was expecting to live with him until I could find work and move into my own apartment. I waited with uncertain anticipation for him to come; since he had disappointed me so many times in the past. However, by the time I had just about completely given up on him, down the road, just ahead of a trail of dust caused by his speeding car, he came for me.

When we arrived in Montgomery, I expected to go straight to his home, but instead he took me to the home of an ex friend of his without even giving her any prior notice that he was bringing me; Only then did he tell me that this was where I would be staying. This friend was a widow woman who lived alone. She seemed to have had some high expectation that the relationship between her and my father would somehow, develop into something more lasting. This of course, turned out to be a great disappointment for her, as the relationship did not turn out that way at all. Before that day, it had been months since she had last seen or even heard from him.

Once we were in the house, he simply said to her in a matter- of -fact way, "This is my son. I want him to stay with you for a while." After a brief exchange of words between them, he left the house. Of course I found myself very uncomfortable being alone, far from home, having been dumped off with a total stranger that was a former friend of his. Her icy stare at me after he had gone only increased my bitter misery, which was obviously shared between the two of us.

After a brief spell she says to me, "Son what did your daddy say to you when he brought you here?" I told her that he didn't say anything to me other than this is where I will be staying. She then informed me of their former relationship, and how long it had been since she had seen or heard from him, and how hurt and disappointed she was because of his shunning her. She at the same time assured me that I was welcome in her home. She told me that I could live there as long as I chose to. Of course, that sort of cracked the ice for me. And I promised her that I would pay such boarding fee as she would charge me as soon as I could find work, as I didn't believe in "free loading" or taking advantage of anyone. She then sat down and began to inform me as to how to maneuver around the city and which bus to catch for the various locations around town. This was the most convenient way to travel since neither of us had a car, and to go by taxi would have been far too expensive for me.

My First Job and Thanksgiving Parade

By then it was late October 1954. I immediately began to catch the city bus into town in search for work. Other times I simply walked, as I was used to doing before I left the farm. I was very happy when my father called one day and informed me that an old retired jeweler and his wife living across the street from where he worked were looking for someone to fire the heating furnace for their home. The old man that had done so for years, had died. I took the job even though the pay was very little, I could barely pay my bus fare to and from work from week to week, and had a meager amount left over to buy food and other necessities that I needed. I was very happy for as little as the pay was it was sizably more than I made while working on the farm.

During the month of November as Thanksgiving approached, the elderly lady who was the cook for the family asked me, "Son you are going down town to the parade on Thanksgiving aren't you?" I asked her, "What parade?" She said. "Us Colored people take over the city every Thanksgiving." Of course she was referring to the parade that preceded the rival football game between Alabama State Teacher's College and Tuskegee Institute. Needless to say, up to that time, I had never heard of such event.

The great day finally came. Mrs. Ella, the cook, bundled up in her long coat, warm cap and cape, and hurried out of the house screaming to me as she left; "Son I'll see you at the parade. Don't be long or you won't get a good place to stand." I then hurried and finished my work and took off for down town about three or four blocks away. Upon arriving at Court Square, Boy, was I in for the surprise of my life. As

61

far as I could see in both directions were walls and walls of black people stretching multiple layers deep, on both sides of Dexter Avenue from Court Square all the way to the Capital building on the top of the far away "Goat Hill" on which the white domed capital complex set. From the Square in the opposite direction as far as you could see and all around the curve, they stood on both sides in equally deep layers. I didn't know that there were so many colored people in the whole state let alone in the city of Montgomery. The festival atmosphere that existed throughout the crowd simply lifted me out of this world. For the first time I felt a sense of importance as I stood amidst that seemingly, endless sea of black humanity. This was far too much for a country boy fresh from the farm to expect.

Then came the parade, with miles and miles of well-dressed kindergarten, elementary, high school and college bands, with all kinds of musical instruments and performers walking with perfect precision. Some bands were dancing to the note of every tune that they played, from the "Huckle Buck" "The Be Bop" to the "Funky Broadway" along with several other tunes that were the top hits during that time. There were also beautifully designed and brightly colored floats carrying gorgeous young ladies. Some were dressed in flowing evening gowns, while others were arrayed in scanty bathing suits that were far too little clothing for them to be wearing in the chilly November weather. Handsome, well-dressed male escorts were imposingly perched on each float beside them. Other attendants stood in groups about the floats continuously waving at the crowd as they slowly crept down the hill from the State Capital building toward Court Square.

There were shinny cars and several groups of loud motorcycles with riders who were dressed in glittering leather suits studded with metal rhinestones from their necks to their boots. Those roaring machines were often circling along the wide street bordered by the walls and walls of excited onlookers. There were also men riding fine fast horses adorned with exquisitely decorated harnesses and saddles. They reminded me of the "wild west" movies that I had often seen from the upstairs section of the little movie house in down-town Orrville before I left the plantation. There were many celebrities walking and waving along the parade route, prominent doctors, lawyers, principals, pastors of some of the larger churches, some of whom would distinguish themselves as leaders in the struggle for civil rights a few months later. Scores of other colored men and women who had somehow, made lasting contributions through their service to their communities, their cities or areas which they represented, were also in the parade. Intermingled with them were some persons who had done nothing so noble, but for some unknown reasons, were just glad to be alive and in the crowd. So they joyfully waved or even clowned as they walked, or ran waving to the crowd along the way. Some were pretending to beat drums while others pretended to play invisible horns as they made their way down the long parade route. Whatever the case, everyone seemed overwhelmed with joy and literally having a lot of fun. I could only compare it to a Saturday night ho-down in what now seems far away, Orrville, a place which except for a few brief visits, I had forever left behind.

And just when I thought that I had seen it all, one of the large rival bands marched gallantly onto the Square, with the other one, just as big, waiting closely behind for its chance to compete for the musical and performers mastery of the "Turkey Day" parade. (As it was later called) Rows and rows of uniformly dressed band members moved lively upon the scene playing their various musical instruments as they swayed briskly into the wide open space near the huge fountain which was a permanent fixture in the square. The drum major moved ahead of them stepping like a five-gaited Tennessee walking horse, the type of horses which were raised and trained on the plantation for showing in horse shows around the south. His swift movement reminded me of an African witch doctor often seen in Tarzan movies that were often shown in the nearby town or seen in some of the popular magazines that was circulated around the school before I graduated from high school several months earlier. His swift movements with his cape flying in the breeze, beating the air with his long baton while he mesmerized the crowd directing the band in tunes of popular music that were not usually played by college marching bands. Simply for a good twenty minutes or more, they worked the crowd. Many people in the crowd joined in the swaying, dancing, and singing the songs of the tunes that they were playing. Even Mrs. Ella, the cook, standing not far from where I stood, swayed briskly to and fro with the lively tunes as they were played. When they were finished, the rival band came on the scene trying to out do their competitors that had just gone before. Needless to say, I left that parade that day with a new and larger concept of myself as a country boy living in the capital city of Montgomery, Alabama.

Going Home for Christmas That First Year

By the time Christmas came, a month later, I had saved enough money to buy a nice set of gold-trimmed china dishes for the family. Having waited until the last minute to shop, I had to literally wade through a sea of pressing humanity in order to buy the gift. But I was determined that absolutely nothing short of death or some serious injury would prevent me from buying that gift to take home to Orrville in time for Christmas. After waiting for seemly hours to buy it, it seemed to take twice that long to get it gift-wrapped. So I waited, for everything had to be just right when I catch the bus for home the next day. And I couldn't wait to see the expressions on the face of mother and all the children when I arrived at home bearing a gift that everyone could use. Although I had been gone for only a couple of months, it seemed as if I had been gone for years. Boy was it ever so good to be back home again where everyone made me the star attraction, at least for that Christmas.

Getting home somewhat late on Christmas Eve, I thumbed a ride from Orrville to the house. When I arrived I knew just what to expect. As always, Mr. X never settled (paid them for their year's work) with the sharecropper farm hands until around mid-day Christmas Eve. (This was totally uncalled for since the harvest was completed since late October or the first of November at the latest.) Naturally, this practice created added tension for our mother and the rest of the workers on the plantation who had children for whom they had to shop on Christmas Eve. To make matters worse, they had to get on the back of a canvas-covered truck and head for Selma some fifteen miles away to hastily shop for toys and clothes for the children to have a Christmas that was considered half decent and would fulfill our high expectation that Santa Claus would remember us for our hard work and for having been good all year. Of course, nothing would have been so heart wrending and disappointing for us than to have awakened on Christmas morning and discover that Santa had not visited us during the night.

Our Christmas morning surprises never included any big-ticket items such as bicycles, scooters or roller skates. (Our mother could not afford the first two and we had no sidewalk to make use of the roller skates even if we would have gotten them.) Instead in our "shoe boxes" we always found a couple of apples; oranges; a small box of raisins; some hard peppermint candy; a few packs of firecrackers; a couple sticks of sparklers or Roman candles and one toy, plus an item or two of clothing. One year I got a pair of rubber boots and a flashlight. I couldn't wear the boots on Christmas, since it was a fair morning with no rain in sight. By night, however, I had run the batteries dead in the flash light, leaving me to grope in the dark even as early as that same Christmas night. One Christmas, by the time night came we had busted the head of one of Baby Sister's doll's just to see what caused it to close its eyes when lying down and opened them when it sat up. Of course by the time mother finished with us that day we thought it best not to burst doll heads anymore. All these things rushed back into my mind as I neared the house that Christmas Eve proudly bearing the gift that I had stood so long in line to buy the day before.

Upon arriving at the house, just as I expected, mother was not there to greet me, as the truck had not yet returned from Selma. But the children were all there waiting for me with wide eyes and happy faces. I had informed them by letter as to when I expected to arrive. But most of all, they were awaiting our mothers return from what would prove to be, her biggest shopping trip of the year.

The unwired house was traditionally decorated as it had been year after year as long as I could remember. There were wild green vines draping the two front doors, and the doors between the rooms of the house. A few sprigs of mistletoe gathered from trees in the nearby forest was hanging here and there about the house, having been hung by different children who had read in some magazine or had learned from someone at school, about the part that these items played in the decorating of the home for this Yuletide celebration. The sweet aroma of home baked cakes and potato pies tantalizingly drifted through every room of the house. This aroma will be intensified by the smell of fresh appless and oranges brought home by mother upon her return home from Selma or the local store located in our little town of Orrville. Later that night the smell of the celery-seasoned turkey or hen baking in the kitchen stove across the ramp that joined the house and the kitchen, would dominate these smells. But the warmth of being near the family cheered our hearts and brightened our spirits more than words can ever express.

From time to time throughout the day, the noisy chatter of the excited children was interrupted by loud outburst of one or more of them singing in tuneless tone:

"Jingle Bell, Jingle Bell, Jingle all the way,

Oh what fun it is to ride in a one horse

Open sleigh."

After a brief spell another would commence to sing assisted only by a singer on the battery powered table-model radio on a table in the adjacent room:

> "Here come Santa Claus,
>
> Here come Santa Claus right
>
> down Santa Claus lane.
>
> Hang up your stockings
>
> Say your prayers,
>
> for Santa Claus is coming tonight."

This way they passed the time as they waited for the truck to arrive, not caring whether they got the verses of the songs right or not.

The truck arrived much later than we expected. As usual, mother was tired and hungry when she returned. After we had a snack and a brief exchange of greetings and meaningless conversations, mother prepared to cook the next day's Christmas dinner. The children all went to bed to sweat the night away with their heads covered beneath the heavy quilts and blankets. They tried to force themselves to sleep, while anxiously anticipating the goodies and gifts that would greet them on Christmas morning just a few hours away.

I remained up with mother while she cooked to keep the fire burning in the stove and to help her distribute the fruits and toys that she had brought back from her Selma shopping trip. We distributed them into the shoeboxes that the children had saved all year for this purpose.

Boy, how glad I was to be back home, especially at this Christmas time, smelling the tantalizing aroma of fresh bakeries in the screened-door safe that was used to store the freshly cooked pies and cakes; to hear the familiar sounds of country fowls and farm animals with which I have been so used to hearing all of my growing up years on the plantation. There were bellowing calves, mooing cows, and crowing roosters, all of which made me feel so welcome. But most of all, it was good to be back home with the family again and relive those childhood years as a child once more.

As we sat and talked after the distribution of the fruit and toys in the shoeboxes that were saved by each child for that purpose, I could not help reflecting on the skimpy little un-lit, poorly trimmed and just as poorly decorated Christmas tree that stood in one dark corner of the room. It stood there with a pile of fluffy cotton at its base serving as snow, a few ropes of assorted colored garlands, and a few handmade ornaments. The tree was barely visible in the dimly lighted room that was poorly flooded with light produced by a single kerosene lamp with a clean pregnated globe that sat on a nearby table. It was most insufficient in providing enough light for reading, even though down through the years this was the only source of light that we had other than that furnished by the narrow fireplaces by which we lived, studied, and played during the chilly summer and bitter cold winter's nights. But tonight, somehow, with me having so quickly become used to the bright electric lights of the city, it was no longer sufficient to meet my need for reading or doing other close-up work. However, dim as it was, it was more than bright enough for me to see the tiredness and anxiousness on mother's face as she tried to relax from the gruesome task that she had experienced during the day. Perhaps her tiredness was mostly due to her hard work in the cotton field during the year, especially during the harvest that had just ended. I could not help but pity her for having to work so hard in the field. The backbreaking tasks of picking cotton, and dragging the long sacks which when full, by far outweighed her, were very devastating for her to say the least. She then would have to carry the full sack on her back and shoulders to baskets across the long rows and tall stalks far down the field to empty it into a woven wood basket. She would then climb into the basket to pack the cotton down in order to maximize the use of the basket. This action was repeated through out the day until the harvest was completed. Knowing this caused me to renew my determination to move her from this overwhelming and oppressive country life as soon as it was humanly possible.

We finally concluded our conversation and late night chores, by saying our good nights, and drifting apart to retire for bed in different rooms of the house, amidst snoring children on the inside, and crowing roosters outside in the nearby hen house. Those sounds reminded us that the mid-night hour was upon us, and the Christmas dawn was about to break.

Christmas Morning Finally Comes

The flapping wings and solemn crowing of "Old Faithful" the rooster, from the nearby henhouse, interrupted our brief night's sleep telling us that the long-awaited Christmas Day had finally come. After stirring the still-glowing coals and rekindling the fires in the fireplaces, the children all got up to see and compare what Santa had left them while they slept.

However, their Yule-tide celebration would come to an abrupt standstill and they all would sit around like stone statues, daring to move a muscle as mother commenced to carry out the age-old family tradition of kneeling on the side of her bed and praying aloud in a most lamentable tone, giving thanks to the Lord for all the blessings he had afforded us during the year. She would call each child by name as she openly prayed for us all. There was always a feeling of sadness in our hearts by such prayer, but we got up each Christmas morning year after year, knowing just what to expect. For this was a tradition that had been the practice of Mama Lillie, as long as I can remember even to the year before she died. She, too, rising early and kneeling on the side of her bed would pray aloud and long. During those years our mother, her children along with her sister, Mary, and her children, (before they moved out,) sat as we now sat and felt the sadness that we now feel, when Mama Lillie called their names in prayer along with all their children. Today each child waited and listened for his or her name to be included in mother's prayer on this special Christmas morning. I, too, waited and felt somewhat special, in that she did not forget me as she prayed for everyone else. Moreover, she prayed that the Lord would give me special favors and blessings during the coming year, as I continued to pursue plans to move them from the farm. When the prayer was over the children with great excitement resumed their delightful task of opening and comparing the gifts and goodies found in their shoeboxes that bore their names. Toys or items too large for the boxes were neatly piled beside them.

It never failed, as long as I can remember, someone always interrupted our Christmas celebrations when some child or even a grown-up from the plantation would come by, and thinking that they had seen us first, would call out to us, " Christmas Give" They expected to receive some sort of gift for having seen us before we saw them. An apple, an orange or some other small gift was usually sufficient to satisfy them for having seen us before we saw them. Sometimes they only got was our reply "Give it to me".

However, all this was done in the spirit of fun and joy of the season and no one was affected one way or the other by our response, or whether they received a gift or no gift.

Like no other Christmas, I once again became a child as I waded through the toy-strewn floor, which was cluttered with almost every kind of cheap toy that eight small children could wish for. There were dolls, cap pistols, a plastic baby grand piano, guitar, drums, small wagons, firecrackers, sparklers, roman candles, and many other toys and items of clothes that seemed to have made all the children very happy. By evening, I was as worn out from playing with the toys as the children were to whom they belonged.

With the coming of night, the children all seemed somewhat sadden. It was a sadness which I always felt, as a child, knowing that the long-awaited day had come and gone. Like I used to do, they all commenced to count the number of days before the next Christmas would be upon them. Any way we looked at it, it would seem like an eternity. I would be another whole year of a laborious growing season along with a backbreaking harvest with an all too often interrupted, school attendance in between. These were their thoughts as they one-by-one said their prayers and their goodnights and went quietly off to bed.

Two days later, I would head back to Montgomery in search for a better job so that I would be better prepared to move the family away after the next harvest season was ended. With that the Christmas season was over for us, and life rapidly returned to its normal humdrum drudgery as it was before.

Back in Montgomery, I remained at work firing the furnace for the old couple for about another month, when out of the blue, they informed me that they no longer needed my service. This indeed was a heart-breaking experience for me, even though the job hardly paid enough to help me with the things that I needed the most. It was at any rate, my first job and it did hurt very badly having lost it. After all I was able to afford the cost of a bus ticket back home for Christmas and buy a set of dishes for the family as well, without this little job neither would have been possible for me.

With no job, I thought this was an opportune time for me to investigate the possibility of joining the military. I informed our mother of my plan to help her through this effort. She reluctantly accepted the idea. I therefore made one more trip to Orrville to take my clothes and other possessions as I prepared for my induction. Our mother later informed me of her sadness that resulted when she considered that I was willing to join the military in order to help them leave the plantation.

To keep my appointment with the recruitment officer a few days later, I returned to Montgomery, only to learn that I had been placed in the "4-F" class and did not meet the qualification for joining the military at that time. Of course, I immediately concluded that this was due to Mr. X having fixed it so well while I was still on the farm. I also concluded that he "un-fixed" it promptly after I had moved my family from the plantation, for at which time I was immediately placed in the "1-A" category, and would be drafted into the army less than two years later.

Once again I returned to Montgomery to search for work. Day after day I would beat the bushes, going from door to door, and from factory to factory, or going just about anywhere that I thought that I might be able to find work. I did all this only to discover that no help was needed. Then just short of panic, I resorted to a private employment service, which charged an extortious fee to provide jobs that only people who were desperate for work would have.

After about a month of searching and waiting, I was finally sent to work for an ice making and banana distributing company in a run-down section of down town Montgomery. As might be expected; the work was hard, particularly the handling of the large heavy stalks of bananas, which had to be carried at arms length above the head and shoulder to avoid bruising or crushing them, especially those that were half ripe or turning. On the other hand, the temperature in the ice storage room was simply unbearable, for one could only work in there for short periods of time before emerging to thaw out. Plus the pay was not equal to the amount of hard work that I was expected to do. Therefore I continued to look for a better job even while I worked there.

Finally by the last of November or the first of December, the local State Employment Service sent me across town for an interview to be considered for a job as short order cook at a small drive-in barbeque restaurant and grill. Upon my arrival, the owner, Mr. Paul Sullivan, greeted me with the warmest smile. He was a tall and slightly heavy kind faced man very much unlike most other bosses that I had previously known. He was obviously a Christian gentleman who smiled easily and looked me straight in the eyes while talking with me. Mr. Paul and I immediately bonded and he hired me within minutes after I arrived. Thus a new positive chapter of life began for me. This job would afford me the long-awaited opportunity to move the family from the country to Montgomery. Furthermore, the restaurant was situated within a stone's throw of the city's bus line, which made it very convenient for me to get to and from work for an affordable fare.

Chapter 9

Walking and Working During
the Montgomery Bus Boycott
(December1955-December 1956)

I had been on the job for only a few days when the most phenomenal Montgomery Bus Boycott began on December 5th of that year. So soon my bubble of enthusiasm was burst and my hopeful optimism was dashed to bits. Riding the bus was my only source of transportation, and the restaurant was all the way across town from where I lived.

The first day of the boycott, a very kind white woman who managed the restaurant carried me home, wondering as we drove along if it was safe for her to do so. She repeatedly said that, she had never seen the like of this before. The next day however, she informed me, with tears in her eyes, that due to a conversation that she had with some of the men who frequented the restaurant, she thought it was not safe for her to take me home again. But even then, she wished me well as I walked toward home during the dim twilight hours of the evening.

I understood her all too well, as well as the reason for the boycott, which I supported by staying off the buses through out its entire duration. Even in the short time that I had been in town, I too had questioned why we had to stand behind a white line painted on the floor of busses, and over empty seats while riding on an over-crowded bus that was only going into the black community in the first place. I therefore joyfully walked day after day with the throng of other protestors for the entire duration of the boycott; or at least until I moved too far away, for me to walk to and fro for work.

Our walk was only interrupted by the insistent coaxing of drivers of privately owned automobiles, church owned vans, even taxi drivers, who carried us just about any place that we were going free of charge. We were obliged the same cost-free courtesy while returning home from a hard days work in the evening. I was amazed by the jubilant spirit and sense of comradery that prevailed among each small group of walkers as many of them refused to accept rides offered for free, choosing rather to walk together from one side of town to the other. Only those going distances too far to walk, or those who were rather aged or crippled, accepted rides on a regular basis.

In the meantime, my new boss, Mr. Sullivan, fully supported all that was going on so far as the boycott was concerned. He felt that every one should be treated fair and decently, especially in the city of Montgomery, the capital of the state of Alabama. Furthermore, he felt that my commitment to work toward moving my family from the country was indeed a noble idea. And he pledged his support by promising me all the hours of work that I needed in order to further me along in this effort. All the time I would hear him using his famous optimistic saying no matter how bad things seemed to have been. He always said, "It could always be worse." I think that I unconsciously adopted this saying as my very own statement of encouragement. I am always reminded, even to this day, that no matter how awfully bad things are, "they could always be worse." Church members, friends and acquaintances have heard this statement repeated by me time and time again over the past forty-five years. These words ring just as true today. If I could force you to listen to my awful singing as they have had to, you too would immediately conclude, "things could indeed be worse."

The rest of that year moved rather rapidly for me. I was engaged in getting used to the long hours of working the new job, and constantly meeting new friends as we walked during the early morning hours. Most nights that I worked, I often had to walk alone after getting off at mid-night. - Even during that late and ungodly hour, I had no fear as I walked across town toward the place where I was boarding.

The only harassment or threat that I ever encountered while walking was from the city police one night as I walked through a section of a white neighborhood that bordered the black community. A police car pulled up beside me and one of the men shinning a bright light in my face wanted to know just why was I walking in that neighborhood that time of night. I tried to shield my eyes from the blinding glare with my hand. "Take your damn hand down" he ordered me in a very abusing tone. After I fearfully informed them that I had just gotten off work at Sullys, and was going home.

The Saga of the Muses

They slowly moved on, leaving me to tread the rest of the way unmolested by anyone.

The next morning when I informed Mr. Sullivan about what had happened, he wanted to know, since I couldn't get a name or a badge number, the exact time this incident had occurred? At the same time he assured me that neither those nor any other police would ever even speak to me again no matter what time of night I was passing through that community. Just like he said, from that time forth, I walked peacefully, night after night, with the police simply looking the other way as they passed by.

With the summer fast coming to an end and the harvest season about to begin, an alarm went off in my mind alerting me that it was high time for me to commence looking for a house large enough to accommodate our family. Housing was in short supply, even for a regular size modest apartment, but to find a larger house of size was a most difficult ordeal. After looking near and far through out the city for quite some time, I finally found a group of larger houses being built on the outer skirt of town. It was in a section just outside the city called Greater Washington Park, located about five or six miles from down town Montgomery. Securing the deal with the required deposit, I was assured that we would be the first occupants to be privileged to move in when the construction was completed before the years end.

Having secured a house so far from the inner city, and with the bus boycott still in process, my major problem would be transportation to and from work. I realized that in order to make the transferring of the family work, I would have to move in with them to maximize their possibility for survival. The distance from the house to the job made it next to impossible for me to walk, even if I wouldn't have to work after such long walk. With my meager income along with the anticipated added obligations I couldn't afford to buy a car. So I did the next best thing, I went to the City Pawn shop and bought myself a used bicycle. This was the first and only bike that I ever owned, even though I had longed to have one before I left the country. But, as I said before, that was a big-ticket item that mother could not afford. Now out of sheer necessity, as a full-grown man, I finally have one of my very own.

By the first of December the house was finally ready. I therefore, commenced to make it ready for the moving of the family. I became involved in getting the utilities turned on, and purchasing such small items, as I knew that they would not have previously needed, but would now need. The purchase of any electrical appliance such as a radio, refrigerator, clocks and the like were a must. Since they never had electricity while living on the plantation, they never had the need to possess such items. Gas space heaters, a stove and a hot water heater came with the house. I also had telephone service installed. I felt that it would give them a feeling of comfort and luxury upon their arrival once the moving venture was completed.

Meanwhile, on the farm the family was sacrificing by pinching pennies, making do with old clothes and not buying things for the house that could wait until they moved. Mother was conscientious of the possibility that if she had sought the usual amount of advancements that year, when settlement came on Christmas Eve, Mr. X would employ his usual tactics which he commonly used on workers at settlement time: "You just lack one more bale to become clear of the debt that you owe me." So she worked harder and made greater sacrifices that year than ever before. She was also very concerned that someone knowing of her plans might leak the information to Mr. X, which also would have ended in disastrous results. For if he had been thusly informed, he would by no means announced her clear of debt; and most certainly would not have allowed her to receive the money that she so badly needed for the transition that they were about to undertake.

Well, Christmas Eve finally came. And as usually, Mr. X kept everyone waiting until about mid-day before he commenced to settle with them. Family by family, he would call them into his office to give them the news and such money as they may have cleared, often he was heard repeating to some: "If you had made just a few more bales, you would have just about broken even." Needless to say, any number of them came out of that office with broken hearts and had nothing to show for a whole year of hard work. None were convinced that they had gotten a fair settlement, even though they may have cleared some money. There was always the feeling that something was lacking. Those that had cleared nothing often came out of the office having made a loan on the next year's crop, and with the hope of having a better year than this one turned out to be.

Finally, Mr. X calling mother by her nickname, "Tut Muse," will you come in? Nervously she went in. After inviting her to sit, he said to her. "Tut, you and your children worked very hard this year and it all paid off for you. Y'all made thirty-five bales of cotton, which was by far more than some of the other folks. Plus you kept your borrowing down quite low this year. Therefore, you cleared all your debts, and you will receive three hundred and fifty dollars." When he had finished counting her meager earnings out to her, he once again complimented her for her and her hard -working children.

Mother then asked him, "You say I don't owe you anything?" He with a puzzle on his face answered; "No you don't owe me a damn thing." She said, "Well, since I don't owe you anything, I just want you to know that I am going to be moving." He with a shock on his face said, "What? When?" "I am going to be moving one day next week, she said." "Why? I thought y'all were happy." He said. "Where are you going?" he continued. "My son is moving me to Montgomery," she replied. "You mean old Preacher is moving y'all away?" He asked. Her reply was "Yes sir, he is." Mr. X, obviously shocked, scratching his head, simply said, "Well, I'll be damned."

He then commenced to compromise and make deals with her by promising to have her house wired with electricity, to build for her the promised crib for the storing of the corn which he had dumped in a corner of the kitchen. It without a doubt, created the greatest fire hazard on the plantation. "If you stay I will fix the road that leads to your house and have someone to build the outhouse that you said you needed earlier this year." He continued. Mother simply thanked him and tucking away her little money quietly walked out of his office. This time she didn't catch the truck to Selma with the rest of the farm worker for the annual Christmas Eve shopping spree. In the interest of saving money, she simply caught a ride to our little town of Orrville to do such shopping as was necessary in order for the children to have a decent Christmas the next day.

(M r. X's shock, more than likely, was due to a foregone conclusion that he had fostered over the past few years.

He, in reference to the speculation as to who would be leaving his plantation and who would remain there, was known to have said: "There are two families that I know will always be here. One is Booker T. Powell, and the other is Tutt Muse." The reason he gave was that each family was too large and too dependent on his support for survival, and therefore neither dared to leave. At any rate, he said, "Where can they find a house big enough to accommodate such large families as theirs?" These were the two largest families that lived on his farm. The Powells were renters of several cotton and cornfields that joined those that we worked as sharecroppers. Therefore, on this bleak and cloudy Christmas Eve, Mr. X received the shock of his life when mother sprang this bit of news on him.

During the next few days Mr. X sent different ones from the plantation by to "talk some sense" into her. He realized the seriousness of her intents. They all came by and talked to her. Some were serious about it, while others talked, winking their eyes and telling her, "If your son is sending for you, don't delay your departure, you must go at once."

Christmas morning that year (1955) was more filled with the anticipation of moving rather than thinking of what Santa Claus had brought during the night. This was the case with all but the smallest and youngest of the children. All others were busy packing both large and small boxes; discarding and disposing of things that they didn't think they would need when they arrived in the city. As they busily packed, they found it hard to believe that the long anticipated time was only a few days away. They would soon be saying their final farewells to these all-to-familiar people, places and things that had meant so much to them all the prior days of their lives. Already they found themselves seriously wondering just what life was going to be like when they got to Montgomery. Their raging anticipation was almost more than even the strongest of them could bear. In their hearts, some felt that something would go wrong at the last moment and causing them to remain on the plantation for an unspecified longer period - maybe another year or perhaps for the rest of their lives. Mother's usual Christmas morning prayers were mostly generic offering thanks to the Lord for keeping us throughout the year and asking him for a good crop year the next year. But this Christmas took on a different form. It was dedicated toward thanking the Lord for having brought them to this point in time and beseeching his continued blessings for this great venture on which they were about to embark. This was also the consensus of the prayers uttered by the children who, on other Christmases, were required to pray aloud while kneeling at their bedside or on one of the several chairs scattered about the room. When the prayers ended, the celebration began with special zest and vitality.

89. Lottie and I (around 1957)

610. Mamie & Michael before we married.

#4. Mary Ann's baby picture

Ms. Mary Ann's high school graduation picture.

Edie Sharp from, as an adult.

Chapter 10

Moving Day and the Trip of No Return

Moving day came the next week, and in keeping with mother's plan to move before the New Year. I rented a truck and hired a friend to drive it to the country for them. My landlady volunteered to accompany him since I had to work that day. After I gave them directions, they left early that morning expecting to arrive, load the truck and leave before nightfall. My older sister, who had doubted that this day would ever come, said "when I saw the truck, only then was I convinced that we were really leaving." Reminding me of the Old Testament story of Jacob, who for many years thought that his son Joseph was dead. He even doubted when informed that he was alive in Egypt and was sending for him to leave Canaan to come to Egypt to live. "But when he saw the wagons Joseph had sent for him" he was convinced that Joseph was indeed alive and he rose to go to him." Like so, their seeing the truck with its canvas covered body, and gleaming cab, they were convinced that their longest dream was about to become a reality.

The loading of the truck moved rather rapidly, since mother had sold all the animals and chicken that she owned, even "Old Faithful" the rooster had either been sold or had earlier met his untimely fate by ending up in a pot of chicken and dumplings for one pleasant Sunday afternoon dinner. They had discarded all but the items of furniture; house accessories and things that they felt would be needed when they arrive at their new home in Montgomery. A few people from the farm came by to help with the loading of the larger boxes and the heavier pieces of furniture, and were anxiously collecting for themselves such items as were being left behind. Someone said that even Mr. X, stood on the bed of his pickup truck out on the big road and watched in discust as the last items were placed on the truck, and one by one the smaller children were helped upon the truck for departure. The youngest child and the baby rode in the cab with the driver, mother and my landlady.

After saying their final good byes and exchanging a few hugs and tears, the rest of the children climbed upon the truck. The humming of the truck's engine and a few rocks and bumps of its wheels over the rough end of cotton rows with stubs of freshly cut stalks, still protruding like so many toy soldiers from each row, at the edge of the narrow dirt road. They were finally on their way. On and on they went until the truck finally vanished down the winding dusty road leaving an empty house, some discarded pieces of furniture and a swirling trail of dust as the only reminders that they had ever lived there. Once started, only a God- forbidden tragedy could cause them to return to the plantation that was rapidly vanishing in the distance behind them. For now they will settle for no place short of Montgomery, Alabama as their final destination.

The children all bundled up in heavy coats to ward off the winter's chill, and sitting on chairs that were set in up in a place provided for them on the canvas-covered truck, arranged themselves so that they could peer through the slats of the truck siding to view the exciting scenes along the route. They observed as the dusty gravel road gave way to a narrow strip of smooth riding pavement, the many bumps that had jolted them all the way from the farm were replaced by fewer and fewer clicks and clacks that broke the continuity of the seemly never-ending highway, as they made their way into Selma some fifteen miles on their journey. In the city they listened to the racing sound of the truck's engine as it bounced back toward them from the buildings built so closely together near the street's edge. The different colored traffic lights, even the flashing yellow ones, seemed to be an added attraction for them since they had so seldom visited the city while living on the farm.

Leaving the city of Selma, they couldn't help but notice the "soon to be famous" Edmond Pettus Bridge that spanned the swiftly moving Alabama River that ran many feet below between two high limestone bluffs that were connected by the bridge. The only other crossing was a railroad trestle seen far in the distance to the left. Little did they know that this bridge would find its way into the pages of both National and World history for the part it would play in the struggle, known as "Bloody Sunday" an event which would be waged in the pursuit of their continued freedom, the first leg of which they had just begun as they steadily ventured toward the city of Montgomery, Alabama. They had no way of knowing that the ground on the far end of this bridge would one day be stained with the blood of our people yearning to achieve their rights to vote and to achieve the status of first-class citizenship of this country in which they had worked so long and hard.

On and on the truck rumbled and made its way down Highway 80 East over long and steep hills and winding curves and tree lined highway toward Montgomery. By this time nightfall had overtaken them, and as they peered into the darkness, there was not much to see until they neared the city. Some of them later described the surge of excitement they experienced as they saw the bright-animated neon signs, which showed animated flying birds; walking people; and running animals that seemed to make their way across the signs moving but not really going anywhere. They however, would not have long to bask in their fascinations, for unknown to them, these signs indicated that they were only a few minutes from the site of their new home, just a few miles beyond the airport where they first appeared. They had no way of knowing that this route they had just traveled would also become very famous a few years later as hundreds or perhaps thousands of our people move by foot the entire spanse of fifty miles with the Alabama State Capital as their final destination, in the trek known as the "Selma to Montgomery March" which would begin with the "Bloody Sunday" experience on the "Edmond Pettus Bridge" only a few years later. Nor did they have any idea of the rumor that would claim that some of the horses to be used in this "Bloody Sunday" mayhem would come from the plantation that they had just left, and provided by the generosity Mr. X himself.

Eyes Peering through the Truck-bed Slats

Those last few miles raced rapidly by and before they knew it, the truck pulled up to the brand new house, which would be their home for the next few years. Even though it was built of cinder blocks, the green painted outside made it appear like a dream house to them as they peered through the slats of the truck's body while they waited for the tailgate to be opened so they could disembark and inspect it more closely. My landlady later described this scene to me, (as I having to work the late shift that night, was not able be there to greet them upon their arrival.) She said that she could see nothing but wide excited eyes peeking through the slats when she went toward the back of the just parked truck. Years later, I have attempted to fit each pair of those eyes to the particular face of a child, along with some of the things that they would accomplish as years rolled by.

Two of those eyes were those of our next older brother Nelson, (who after a lengthy bout with a serious illness, would acknowledged his call into the Christian ministry, and for many years would pastor several churches in the Montgomery area and would pastor a sizeable fast-growing and progressive church in the college town of Auburn, in Alabama, where he would successfully pastor for at least twenty two or more years. He would also become a family man with a wife, several sons and daughters and many grand and a few great grand children.)

Two were the eyes of a next older sister, Lucile, (whose caring and compassionate demeanor would compel her to become a "Home Patient Care" nurse, attending to and comforting the elderly, the seriously ill and dying patients during their final hours on this earth. Her compassionate mourning and sincere grieving with family members during the passing of loved ones automatically would lead us to designate her the "Mother Teresa" of the Muse clan. She would continue to serve in this capacity even down to this present day. Her love for this work is only exceeded by her love for her two lovely daughters, a son and her grandchildren.)

Next peering through the space between the slats of side of the just arrived truck, were the eyes of Mary Pearl, another sister, who waited patiently but curiously for the tailgate of the truck to be opened. (While she, like most of the older children, would finish high school but not be privileged to go on to college. Pearl would grow up to become a very profitable textile worker. She would also become a trusted, supportive and stabilizing force in dealing with the many seemingly unending family crisis and emergencies throughout all her years both now and always. Her devoted husband and two lovely daughters and grandson would become the pride of her very fruitful life.)

Two were the eyes of another brother Joe, (who would after acquiring a Bachelor's degree with honors in Math from Alabama State University, even before graduation, would be employed by IBM in the state of New York, traveling extensively from place to place, even to foreign countries, trouble-shooting and repairing computers and other such machines produced by that very impressive company. After a lengthy career in that area, he would move to Charlotte, North Carolina where he would continue to be an active servant of humanity in the city of Charlotte and the surrounding area.)

Another pair of eyes were those of another sister, (Minnie, whose wide eyes and easy tears were indicative of her tenderness of heart, and her over-all alertness and searching eyes often makes one a bit uneasy just being in her company, especially if he or she has the slightest intent of thinking or doing any thing that is not just right. She would attend the Trenholm State Technical School in pursuit of a

---

degree as a "Seamstress," a degree that helped her land a supervisory career at a leading textile firm located across the state and around the country. Her devotion her job will only be exceeded by her love for her husband, their two daughters of par-excellence and an only grandson.)

The last pair of eyes peering through the slats of the truck's side were those of a younger brother, Richard. (Richard was sort of a quiet person who spoke rather rapidly when he did speak to make amends for a slight stutter that he had which also caused him some confusion as he attempted to converse with the other children. It would be quite sometime later that we all would come to know that he had a heart of gold and would do anything to help anybody at any time. He would come to be known for his mechanical skill, for he could rebuild the most complex engine from scratch, taking it apart and putting it together again. He would also enroll in the Trenholm State Technological School, acquiring a degree in Brick Masonry. But his real claim to fame would be his acute acumen of being a caring father of four very smart and lovely daughters, all of whom remained on the honor role through their high school and college years and each would take her place among the elites of the professional world.)

The youngest sister, Ida Bell, who was just a toddler, was gently lifted from the cab of the truck where she and the baby brother, Jimmy, had ridden with the grown-up that traveled with them. They were too young to remember anything about the plantation experience or even the trip that brought them to Montgomery. (Ida Bell would grow up to become a devoted wife and the proud mother of two fine sons and at least one grandson. Her servant spirit will compel her after she finish high school, to enroll at the prestigious Spellman College, in Atlanta, Georgia, from which she would graduate with a degree in English. She would later change careers and become a registered nurse, which enabled her to secure a position as "Disease Control Specialist" at one of Montgomery's finest heath care facilities. Every family need's a Florence Nightingale and Ida Bell is ours.)

Jimmy, the youngest brother of the Muse clan, was hauled from the cab of the truck in the arms of our mother. Even if he hadn't been too young to remember anything about the trip, he was too much asleep to give a hoot at that late hour of the night. (After finishing high school Jimmy would enroll at Alabama State University. Later his exemplary supervisory ability would secure him a career in this area of that responsibility at a leading manufacturing company in the Montgomery area, even though he would become the caring and supportive father of several sons and daughters. He would always occupy the "baby" position in heart of our mother and the entire family clan.)

With this we have put faces on each pair of eyes that peered through the slats of the truck's side as they waited for the tailgate of the truck to be opened, that they might proceed to examine their new found home. The gate having been opened they hurryingly climbed or jumped down from the truck, carrying such small personal item as they could easily carry. After a brief inspection they commenced to help with unloading the truck, setting up the beds as they were brought in. As they worked they could not hide their fascination with the new gas stove and how warm the small gas heaters had made the house in the short time that they had been there. A brand new refrigerator and a telephone that worked only heightened their level of excitement. The truck having been unloaded, it hummed off into the night, leaving them all to themselves to complete the arranging of such furniture as was needed for the night. With this the long awaited family exodus was finally completed. I would join them in our new home after getting off work later that night.

Enduring Challenges in Our Newfound Community

The next several months posed unending challenges for us all. By now, the bus boycott was well under way, which made our adjustment to this transition a bit more complicated. However, my problem of getting to and from work was solved when a former fellow employee insisted that I abandon the idea of riding the bike that I had recently purchased for this purpose, offering to pick me up each morning and even in the evening if I would wait until he got off work about a hour later than I usually got off. Each morning he came as regular as clock-work in his long cloth-top convertible which seemed a bit louder than it should have been. But loud or not, I was very thankful for his most thoughtful and faithful accommodation and the bicycle ride that I would never have to make.

Meanwhile, the family was adjusting more rapidly than I expected. The older children immediately enrolled in school, and for the first time riding the school bus, were able to resume their education without many interruptions. Mother was able to find part-time work as housekeeper at a nearby local motel. While some of the older children went to school and worked part time at such odd jobs as they could fit into their school schedule. Already in a few months the family's income exceeded a year's income that they would have received working on the plantation, thereby giving credence to the idea that they had indeed arrived and settled into the "Promised Land."

We had been there only a short time when we begin to realize some of the many problems that were associated with the community. For instance, because there was no underground drainage system, and with the railroad bordering the lower end of the community, the streets were often flooded with the least amount of rain. However, since we lived on the upper end of the street, we were not affected by it unless we chose to venture about two houses beyond ours, then we too would have to wade in the water. Then there was the problem of a loud vulgar and violent neighbor whose harsh voice could be heard mornings, noon and evenings cursing her very timid and humble husband who took it all without mumbling the slightest word. This trend would only be broken on one dastardly day, as she would end his life with the blast of a shotgun fired into the back of his head at close range.

Other acts of violence were typical in the streets, which were influenced by a local night spot called the "Chicken Shack" located three streets behind our house. While my brother Nelson mixed rather easily with the young men of the community without much difficulty, the same could not be said of myself, for the only night that I accepted the invitation to join them at the club, I came very close to being butchered by a mad man, the "bully" of the neighborhood called "Red". Who chased me with a long switchblade as I ran around a car that I had borrowed with the purpose of buying. Since he didn't cut me as he stood over me after I was down, I concluded that he was only bluffing. But bluffing or not, I never ventured into that area again. And neither did I buy the car that I had borrowed. For who would want to buy a car that had come so close to becoming his tomb? Well, that is one reason that I give for not buying it. But the real reason was that I just couldn't at all afford it.

The other gathering place in the community was the crudely built unpainted cinder block church house located one street behind us, which housed the First Baptist church. They met two Sundays each month during the day, but they met every Sunday night rain or shine. Along with mother and the older children we joined that church, which presented us the opportunity to get to know many of the church going people of the community, as well as to continue our age-old practice of worship, and even more frequently than we ever did before we left the plantation, for there our church met only one Sunday each month. It was while attending one of these meetings that I met Lottie, the young secretary for the Sunday School of the church. She was a tall and slender young lady, with a dark velvet-like complexion and bright coal-black eyes. Little did I know that after a brief period of courting, we would become husband and wife.

Once we were married, she moved in with our family into which she made a perfect fit, for her gala and jubilant personality seemed to bring an air of ease into the worse of situations, and her cackling laugh had the power to make you forget that the house was on fire. Mother and the children accepted and dearly loved her without the slightest reservations whatever. And I even think that she loved them more than she loved me. For some of our earlier marriage conflicts were due to her thinking that I was too rough on the younger children from time to time. And whatever the family had to endure she gladly shared it wholeheartedly as if it was her very own.

Upon finding a larger house that offered us more accommodations closer into the city, we would be moving within the year after our marriage. This move would be the first of three other moves that we would make, before we finally realized that the family had reached such stability as to sort of stand on their own with very little or no assistance from me. We therefore, for the first time, moved out into our own apartment, both of us rather young and quite uncertain about our future and what it would be like living all by ourselves.

It was just before we moved out on our own that I acknowledged my call to the Christian Ministry. After discussing it with Lottie and the family, I was compelled to inform our pastor and the church. A few Sundays later I was preaching from the pulpits of various churches throughout the city and surrounding communities. I even went back to Orrville and preached at my home church there. My announcement of course, surprised neither my church in Montgomery nor my previous church back in Orrville; as for some reason they confessed that they had been predicting this all the time. Needless to say, this was the most influential pivoting point that would determine the mission of the rest of my life. For it would turn out to be that from that time on, in this commitment will "I live move and have my being."

Our mother predicted with amazing accuracy two things that would occur upon my entering the ministry: First she predicted that my dad who had shown absolutely no interest in us at all since the family's arrival, would suddenly become interested in me, since he was a minister of a different denomination than we were, and that he would try to persuade me to join the denomination in which he served as pastor. Surely enough, as soon as he got the word he came by, and just as mom had predicted, he made every effort to get me to change, not only my denomination, but also for the first time ever he advised me to change my last name from "Muse" to his. Whereupon, I immediately informed him that since I had invested so much in the name of "Muse," such as attending and finishing grade and high school, I was baptized as "Muse" and since all of my friends knew me as "Muse"; and since I had recently married as "Muse"; and since my dear mother had raised me as "Muse"; I would not insult her nor fail to honor her by changing my name to his. Furthermore, I told him that at this stage of the game, if he wanted the two of us to have the same name that he would have to change his to mine. Of course, that didn't take well with him at all, as he became quite furious with me and as he stormed out the door, he accused me of having insulted him and he vowed that he would never attempt to advise me again about anything, even though it may be for my own good; Whereupon, I politely thanked him and informed him that if I ever needed him I would look up his number and call him. And with that he sped off into the night leaving me with a great feeling of relief. A few weeks later, he came by again and invited me to preach for him at one of the churches he pastored in a remote rural area several counties away.

Next she predicted that a certain young man with whom I had grown up would as soon as he heard about my new calling, would also announce that he had been called into the ministry, since we were somewhat rivals through out our growing up years. She predicted that his announcement would come months later, although I was not surprised when he made it less than two weeks after mine. Strangely, I have never considered myself a rival of his neither then nor now, as today we have both been in the pastoral ministry for almost a half century.

In time, after moving from place to place, my wife and I finally moved into an apartment in a housing project just a few short blocks from the restaurant where I worked. It was located right across from the football stadium of Alabama State University. This was significant in that many evenings after work, I would spend hours watching and listening to the marching band's rehearsals. This was the same band that had mesmerized the crowd and fascinated me in down town Montgomery at my first Thanksgiving Day parade. And now I could relive those precious and awe inspiring moments over and over again, all while sitting on the front porch of our very own apartment minus of the huge crowd that engulfed my down town experience when first I saw them perform.

It was in these quiet humble surroundings that after several alarming and disappointing false pregnancy announcements, that we were finally assured that this one was for real. We therefore began to make ready for the birth of our first child. This process was well under way, when I received notice from the government that I was about to be examined for the draft into the armed services. It would come at such a time as this when my life was just about to fall into place. For in addition to the expected coming of our child, my ministry was also beginning to take shape. Plus mother and the children were able to stand more on their own, giving me more where-with-all to do some of the things that I always wanted to do but never could quite afford. Why would they be interested in me now, when two years earlier, when I attempted to enlist I did not qualify? I wondered.

Meanwhile, my pastor, the Reverend Joe T. Thomas, informed me of his intent to ordain me in order that it may be listed on my military records upon my induction. For he was sure that once I went for the examination that I would be immediately drafted, and he felt that there would be some lasting advantage for me as a ordained minister. He himself had had this same experience when he was drafted as a ordained minister many years earlier. Arrangement was made for this service and carried out a few weeks later.

Therefore, having been ordained, I waited for the final letter from Uncle Sam, and the final examination, as the previous letter had advised, I started planning for immediate induction into the army. I commenced to vacate the apartment and move the wife back home with her grand parents with whom she had lived all of her life prior to our wedding. Therefore, when the letter came a few days later, I was informed that should I pass the examination that I would be immediately sworn in and would not be returning home for at least sixteen weeks. Well, I passed it and after a brief induction ceremony, was shipped out the very next day, August 5th, 1958, to my first station, Fort Jackson, South Carolina, leaving a very pregnant wife at the mercy of her grand parents to look after her during this very crucial time of our lives.

86. Linda's first grade picture.

#6a. Linda's basic training picture.

#56. Linda, as an adult.

Chapter 11

"In The Army Now"
(1958 – 1960)

Upon my arrival at Fort Jackson after nightfall, needless-to say, I was very nervous and didn't know just what to expect. The bold abrasive act of the soldiers in charge only made things worse. For instance, instead of informing the newly arrived recruits that they were not permitted to smoke in the receiving station; they abused them by violently slapping the cigarettes from their hands. All this, of course, was a bit much for me, a young black man from the deep segregated south. The soldiers in charge were mostly black and the abused newly arrived soldiers were mostly white. Furthermore, the language that they were using as they talked to us was indicative of a deep-seated evil that I had only known by reading terror articles in the "Mad Magazine" that was widely circulated through out the nation.

After marching us to a huge warehouse we were measured and outfitted with a complete ration of army clothing. We were ordered to hold each item high as the moderating soldier called them out. We were then ordered to "Put it in the newly issued duffel bag. This act was repeated over and over again until every item was issued and bagged. After that we were marched off to a large area covered with lines and lines of canvas tents. There we were informed that like it or not, this would be our home away from home for the next eight to ten weeks. We were also told that we might expect the same kind of dwellings when we arrive at our next station for an additional eight weeks of training after basic training was completed.

By now it was well past midnight, and we were assigned double decked bunk beds, metal cabinets and footlockers. After making our beds, we exhaustingly crashed in for a few hours rest. Only to be awakened a few hours later by some screaming sergeant beating the metal bed posts with a tin pan and frightening the living heck out of us. This became a routine ritual that we soon learned to expect morning after morning through out the next eight weeks as we went through the first phase of basic training.

During the next few days in one of the platoon formation, our platoon sergeant, a Hispanic American, informed me that he needed to see me right after the break. Afterward, he said to me, "Muse, as you may know, your records arrived on post several days prior to your arrival, and upon reviewing them we noticed that you are an ordained Baptist minister from Montgomery, Alabama. I like what you all are doing down there. I assume that you know the Reverend Doctor Martin Luther King, am I correct?" I exaggerated as I told him that I did and that I had coffee with him the Saturday before I came into the Army. He said "Don't worry I will be looking out for you while you are here under me." Not fully understanding just what "looking after you" entailed, I never the less, felt rather unworthy of the special favors and consideration I was granted. All because I was an ordained Baptist preacher from Montgomery, Alabama, because of the things that were going on back there which had wide ramifications in the development of the civil rights climate through out the whole United States.

Some of the favors and special privileges that I was afforded were: I was never restricted to post at times as the rest of the enlisted men were, because of some disciplinary action imposed upon them for one reason or the other. For instance they may be restricted to post, for half cleaning their weapon. He would simply say to me "Muse, take cleaning patch put a little oil on it and stick it down the barrel of your rifle and get lost." Then there were times when he disciplined them for not properly cleaning and waxing the barrack floor or cleaning barrack latrines; or for not passing the weekend inspections. Whatever the case, I was always exempted from these disciplinary actions. He always told me to go and visit the hospital or do whatever preachers do on week-end-passes.

Then there were several times, as we sat in out-door bleachers during class sessions, that the instructor told unacceptable jokes or addressed the class by using languages that boarded on vulgarity or humor that inferred discrimination in one way or the other. During the break the sergeant would quietly make his way over to the instructor's stand and whisper into his ear. When class resumed, he would publicly apologize to me for having done so in my presence. On the live hand-grenade range he made sure that the sergeant assisting me knew who I was and where I was from. After we went into the throwing pit and I almost threw a fatal grenade, the soldier told me, "Soldier, where ever you go, if you have to throw a hand grenade, you tell those in charge that Sergeant Bill from Fort Jackson, South Carolina, says "don't ever let you handle a live grenade again, but that they should be contented to let you just pray for those that must throw them." Needless to say, because of all these favors and special privileges, I turned out to be a lousy U.S.A. fighting man and did not learn to do anything as well as I should. But I am very thankful never the less. I am thankful, first, to my pastor for his deep wisdom and knowledge shown in having me ordained prior to my entering the service. Then I am most thankful also to my caring and concerned platoon sergeant who actually kept his word by "looking after me" throughout my basic training experiences. By now many of my fellow soldiers, while respecting me dearly, began to take notice and show a bit of envy for the way that I was singled out and treated. Some accused me of being a regular old "brown nose" while most of them delightfully joined the platoon sergeant in protecting me beyond that which I deserved.

By the end of September, we were coming to the completion of our basic training session. We began winding down our activities at this company and began making ready for transfer to our next station. Many of the men began speculating as to just how I would be treated at our next company. Some even betting that I wouldn't fare quite as well, while others concluded that the platoon sergeant had already been in communication with our future platoon sergeant and that it would be very interesting to see just how he would comply with his recommendations concerning me.

The first week of October, our graduation activities from Basic Training were held amidst great pomp and excitement. Our company, platoon after platoon marched with great precision behind a military brass band as we passed in review before high ranking military officers and other civilian guest, who had come on post just for this celebration. Of course we were very proud of our accomplishment during these eight weeks of training. With this, the first leg of our military journey was complete. Now we were to move on to face the challenge of the next eight weeks of advance training. We were immediately moved on to our new camp, which was not very far from our present camp. It would be our home for the next eight to ten weeks. Instead of canvas tents, the barracks were permanent two story structures with all the modern conveniences such as working showers, gleaming polished title floors, central air and heat, and furniture that was of a slightly higher quality than that we had left behind.

During our first formation, after our arrival, the commanding officer and other company staff greeted and welcomed us before leaving us in the hands of our new platoon sergeant. He was a medium short sergeant first class who smiled cunningly out one side of his mouth while the other side remained unmoved but for his most hilarious out burst of laughter. His flashing blue eyes reminded me of those of Mr. X back on the plantation, which to me was a sure clue that he was not to be trusted. His accent was evident that he was from the mountainous area of Tennessee or northern Georgia, and that he could as well had been a close associate with some descendents of the infamous Hatfields and McCoys before he joined the army. One could tell by his gleaming spit-shinned boots, his well-pressed fatigues and polished brass that he was a gun-ho proud career soldier and had no doubt participated in at least two previous military conflicts. Therefore I knew right away that I would have to become a better soldier than I had previously been if I were, in any way, going to get along with him.

During the assembly, I was somewhat surprised when he abruptly informed us that our former platoon sergeant, Sgt. Delray, had informed him that we have an ordained minister among us. He then in his next breath said, "Whoever you are, will you please step forward?" Of course, all the enlisted men looked back at me, and I looked back as if I too was looking for him also. He then said, "Private Muse, step forward." I quickly made my way to the front of the formation and as I stood before him at attention, he said to me, "At ease Private," he continued, "I want you to know that in this company we will respect you in every way, and we will never do anything to reflect negatively against you nor your profession. But In this man's army there will be many things happening that you may not agree with, but you will have to grin and bear them." He closed by saying, "fall back in line"…"Platoon dismissed."

The next few days the company organized the troops into various squads and groups to perform certain duties that were necessary for our functions and wellbeing during this phase of our training. The platoon sergeant requested that we look among us and find responsible men to become acting leaders for the duration of this course of training. They were to be appointed during the next morning's formation. Well the next morning came and during the formation the sergeant called for the selected names. The first name called was a professional football player, Pvt. Don Blendenton, who was taking basic training with us before returning to his N.F.L. team. He was the soldiers' choice for acting sergeant. My name was next; I was selected to become acting corporal during this time. Well, when my name was presented, the platoon sergeant immediately objected to it, and told them that no preacher could possibly be an acceptable acting corporal of the platoon. He then asked me, "Private Muse, if a fellow soldier was brought before you for an offence that you were not sure that he had committed, would you be able to make him work in the grease pit all day and be able to sleep that night?" I told him, "No". With that, he declared that he would not accept either of their recommended persons for those positions, and that he would make known his own choice the next morning.

The next morning came and while standing before the formation, the sergeant commences to name his choice for acting officers. The first name called was "Pvt. Don Blendenton," and then he called "Pvt. Willie Muse." With this I said, I thought that you said that I was not a good choice for this position. He then said, "Soldier, are you questioning my choice for my platoon? I happen to know who I want to serve in this capacity; do you have a problem with that?" With this, Blendenton and I would be privileged to move into the room reserved for officers located on the second floor at the entrance of the barrack. We had responsibilities to look out for the welfare and the immediate needs of the troops of our platoon.

Blendenton and I got along quite well most times. However, many times he openly treated me rather harshly. I think that he may have been partly joking around with me. On the other hand, he may have reacting negatively to the sheer respect that the rest of the troops showed toward me. Whatever the case, from time to time, he belched out loud curse words at me, and told me that he was going to kick my butt. He continued this abusive verbal assault until one day a hairy, burly white soldier came by our room and confronted him by saying, "Don Blendenton, from time to time we have heard you cursing at Muse. Well, we don't curse him nor do we curse around him. Therefore, the very next time we hear you curse at him, we are going to stretch your long tall a." He then rose and left the room. Pvt. Don was shocked beyond words for a while. Once composed, he said to me, "Did you hear what that "Red Neck" said to me? What have you been doing with them? You know that I was just kidding around with you, but I am convinced that those Klansmen will lynch me about you." Well, I think that he got the message. After that, he never even cursed at me nor even around me again during the continued duration of our tour together there. He remained in training with us until those eight weeks were over. He then left to resume his position with his football team with the NFL, giving me the thumb's-up sign and a sneaky one-eye wink. He wished us well as he left us in the army while he returned home to serve in his home state National Guard Service.

By our second week in our new camp I received a telephone call that the time for the baby's arrival was within days and that Lottie, my wife could be entering the hospital any day, or even any hour soon. I was convinced that this was a serious enough situation to warrant my getting a pass from training to go home. I therefore approached the platoon sergeant about the matter and he arranged for me a meeting with the commanding officer of our company. When I related my desire to him, he said to me, "Soldier, it has been proven over and over again, that a man does not need to be present for his wife to have a baby." He then added, "They have some of the best doctors back home whose business it is to assist women in child birth." With this he politely saluted and dismissed me from his presence. As cold as his expression was, it was once again proven that he was correct. A few days later, October 9th, our healthy and lovely daughter Linda, made her début on this earth. I would get to see her for the first time during a two weeks leave for Christmas, two months later that year.

The days leading up to Christmas crept along at a snail's pace, as I greatly desired to see our new daughter. But, creeping or not, the time came and I couldn't wait to get home. Once home, and after a period of cuddling and bonding, time fled by. Before I knew it, it was time to return to post for the final weeks of training, which ended by the last of January. We were immediately shipped by Grey Hound bus to Fort Dix, in New Jersey, for deportation by ship to an ammunition depot in Tois Fountaine, France, sometime early in February.

Upon arriving at Fort Dix, we were given temporary housing as we waited to be shipped off to Europe. Almost exactly as if it had been passed down from camp to camp, I once again was asked by the sergeant in charge to remain after the other troops had been dismissed from formation. He then, like my first platoon sergeant, informed me that they had our records in hand for several days before we arrived. He too, had noticed that I was an ordained minister from Montgomery, Alabama. Like the previous sergeant, he told me how pleased he was with what the people in Montgomery were doing in regards to our protesting unjust discriminatory laws against our people. He then asked me "How well do you know Dr. Martin Luther King?" "I know him very well," I said, "in fact I had coffee with him just before I left the city" I told him, stretching the truth a bit. Even though I did know Dr. King, we were never so close as to have had coffee together. But I was saying what I knew he wanted to hear me say. "Well" said he, "We always look out for our ministers when they come through here, and with you being an ordained minister of the same church as Dr. King, and from Montgomery, and there are some people in key positions on this post that I would like for you to meet." He continued, "Have you ever been on a ship before?" When my reply was "No." he said "Man its hell on a ship any time you cross the ocean on one. But it is even worse when you travel it during the months of February and March. Tomorrow I will take you to meet someone who may be able to change your mode of travel." So we agreed to get together the next afternoon after he got off duty.

The next evening I joined the sergeant in his long sleek convertible Pontiac sedan. This car had a tall swaying rear-mounted antenna that connected to a rare, citizen band radio on which he frequently communicated with someone within his circle of friends as we traveled. Again he repeated how proud he was of the people in Montgomery, and how much he appreciated the Reverend Doctor Martin Luther King, for the leadership that he was providing for our people, not only in Alabama, but through out the nation as well. We rode across the fort until we finally came to the transportation office. Upon entering, we were warmly greeted by a medium built fair complexion black army colonel, who smiled very broadly as he shook my hand. He then informed me that the sergeant had told him about me and that he had anxiously looked forward to meeting me. He then assured me as to how proud he was for what the people were doing in Montgomery. He added, "You people without doubt will change this nation." He then stated, "As an ordained Baptist minister, I am sure that you had some fellowship with Dr. King when you were in Montgomery. Perhaps you two had coffee together on some occasions?" Again, stretching the truth as before, I said, "Sure we had coffee just before I left for the Army." He then stated that he had a copy of my shipping orders, and that I was schedule to depart by ship on Thursday morning of the next week. However, he said, "Like the sergeant and I discussed, we don't want our ministers going overseas by boat. Therefore, if you don't mind traveling by yourself, I can arrange for you a flight to Rhine-Maine airport in Frankfort, Germany, and you will have to take a train across to Bar-le-duke, France, which you shouldn't mind for you will be traveling first class. Once there a limo will pick you up to ferry you to post at Troi Fountaines. If you think that you would like this travel plan and would sign this form you can consider it done," he said. Of course, I gladly signed the form. "We won't be able to change the printed orders," he said, 'therefore, on Thursday morning your name will be called along with the other enlisted men, but all you do when it is called is holler "Scratch" They will be mustered out that day, and you will leave two days later, but don't worry, when they get there, you will have been there for several days."

Just as the officer said, the departure of the troops came and I was left alone for two days after they left. On the third day I was informed to be packed and ready for departure at 0700. I was driven to the airport and boarded a MATS (Military Air Transportation Service) plane for travel. Of course I was very excited and somewhat afraid as this was the very first time I had ever even been on a plane, not to mention flying on one. I was therefore, a little reluctant to put all my weight down as I flew over the ocean. And it didn't help me at all to discover that the seats on the plane were facing the rear and we were literally flying backward. Even so, I was thoroughly convinced that this was far better than sailing on the rough seas as the rest of the men of my company were doing.

The Saga of the Muses

I was simply amazed at the accuracy of my itinerary from the departure; our stop in the Azores; and our timely arrival at Rhine –Maine, in Germany. I was then swished off to the train depot and boarded a train for travel across the Alps for Bal-le duke, France, some twelve to fifteen hours away.

I arrived at Bal-le-duke, around midnight and immediately commenced looking for my transportation to my home post. I went to the ticket county and using my Franco/English dictionary, I sought information about transportation to post. All I got from the attendant was "Je' no comprende" or something that sounded like that. For the first time I felt so all alone being some three thousand miles from home lost and not being able to communicate with the people of that country. I then decided that whenever I got to post that I wouldn't leave it until I was able to at least speak some of the local language.

Sometime between midnight and three o'clock, my heart was made to leap for joy when I heard the powerful roar of a large twin/coach army bus screeching to a stop in front of the depot. It had no more than stopped when a tall U.S. soldier came in and in a loud voice called "Private Willie L. Muse." By then I had concluded that was the sweetest name this side of heaven. Although I had been in travel for less than two days, it seemed as if it had been weeks since anyone at all had called my name.

Once on post, I was assigned living quarters and had nothing to do until the arrival of the rest of the company, which turned out to be more than a week later. During that time I passed the time by visiting the library and reading up on the history of France. I had very little interest in French history while I was in high school and on the plantation back home. I also spent much time in the snack bar and the post hobby shop. There I learned to paint landscapes of scenes that I had seen along the rail route that I traveled between Germany and France. All the time I was wondering just how the rest of the men were faring on their journey upon the high seas.

On or about the eighth day after my arrival, they finally arrived on post. Different ones began to share with me the horrors of their trans-Atlantic experience. These horrors were evident by their drained and exhausted appearance and condition. Their faces were bleached and drawn, their eyes were sunken and most of them professed to have lost several pounds due to their lack of ability to eat or retain the food they had eaten during the long rough sea voyage.

Their sharing of these experiences convinced me that, our Divine Heavenly Father because of his infinite fore knowledge, knew that I would not have survived this passage at this time of year by boat. He therefore, intervened on my behalf and saved my life. The fact that I would not have survived would certainly be validated some eighteen months later upon my return trip home by ship during the month of August, the calmest of summer. On that trip I became seriously seasick on our second day out and remained thus the whole of the nine-day voyage. Also in recent years having attempted to venture in deep-sea fishing, several times I became so sick until I couldn't even put a hook into the water. Once on land I concluded that venturing on the seas would never even become my least pasttime.

The next few weeks we were settling in on our new post. Our area of responsibility as a Light Vehicle Delivery company was to support troops on the battlefield by delivering supplies of ammunition to them. We were therefore stationed near an ammunitions depot just outside of Trio Fountaines, France. Since I could use the typewriter,

119

The Saga of the Muses

I was immediately assigned an office job assisting the Driver's testing non-commissioned officer in charge of Driver's Testing and Training Center. This center handled the training and testing needs for four to six companies from at least three military posts in addition to our own. This position provided far more advantages for me than that of a Light Vehicle Driver, the position for which I was trained at Fort Jackson. I even tested and licensed the men of my company who by now had become like family to me since we had been together since basic training. In this position I would get to know both officers and enlisted men along with their dependants. As they came into France from the United States, they would have to get their driver's licenses updated through a series of training such as becoming familiar with the European traffic signs and local rules of the highway. Therefore, if they wished to drive a motor vehicle whether military or civilian, they had to come to us for training and testing. As previously stated, our office served a four-post area, which included three other nearby posts and ours. I became sort of a favorite soldier to some and a most resented to others on our post. I took my work very seriously as there was a very high incidence of traffic fatality among Americans, both military and civilians in our command. This was due largely to the many narrow and winding tree-lined highways, the reckless and rapid driving habits of the local citizens and the differences of highway laws of France as compared to those of the United States. While my experiences were many and varied, only the following three of my most memorable ones will I detail in this account:

The first experience was an on-going conflict with the post's Adjutant General who was in charge of the Military Police in that area. He would send newly arrives to us with an order to get them licensed whether they passed the written exam or not. When several of them failed I would send them back to him unlicensed. He would send them back to me with orders for me to license them and send them back to him in thirty minutes. I informed my superior officer of it, and he told me to send them back to him and he would take care of it.

The very next day I was visited by an army Colonel from Verdun who informed me that he had come to investigate the problem that I had with the Major. He then complimented me for the reduction in highway fatalities on the post that were assigned to us for training and testing. He further indicated that while he was not sure that we made the difference, he couldn't help but notice that this reduction began around the same time that we began working in this position, and that he didn't want anyone to interfere with this success. He then informed me that he couldn't demand that I do so, but if I would sign a certain form that he had brought with him, I would not be bothered with the Major again. So I signed it and like he said, he never bothered me again the entire remaining time that I was in that position. Nor was I ever placed in his "little black book" as my superior officer had previously warned.

My next most memorable incident involved a civilian, a soldier's wife who happened to be a "White" small town girl from one of the southern states of the United States. She came in and took the test and missed passing by a few points, which I was about to waive, until she asked, "What do I do now "boy?" I barked back "You can come back and take the test again madam." This scenario went of for two or three times repeatedly, until one day her soldier husband came by to see me. He apologetically informed me that he had told her that he knew me and it must be something that she was doing that prevented her from getting her licenses. He then asked me what it was that she was doing or saying to me that kept ticking me off. I informed him that apparently his dear wife couldn't read well enough to drive, since she keeps mispronouncing my name, for she always says "Boy" instead of "Muse" when reading the name written in bold letters on my shirt. He then said, "Muse, I knew that she was doing or saying something that she shouldn't. You see, she is from the south and has never been anywhere else until she came here. "I promise you, that she won't make that mistake again," he said. She came in the next day and apologized to me assuring me that she meant no disrespect at all to me. Thereupon, without any further exam she received her license. I also gained lasting friends in her and her husband for the rest of the time we spent on that post, even though we were from two different companies in the area.

My final most memorable position related incident was after I had brought my wife and baby over to be with me during my tour of duty. We lived on the local economy in the little French village of Revigny, about ten miles from post. There also lived three other Black families either there in Revigny or nearby villages. We maintained a rather cordial relationship from family to family, visiting each other from time to time and often going to the movies or shopping together. Well, one of the wives wanted to get her driver's licenses, as her husband had just bought a new car. She arranged for the necessary training whereupon after the completion she would be given both the written and the road test. As expected, she passed the written test with an above average score. Then the time came for the road test, during which she kept asking about our daughter, Linda, adding how cute she thought she was and how smart she seems to be. Of course, as examiner I just sat and checked her points and demerits as I gave instructions as to what I wanted her to do. When the test was over she asked me "Just how did I do?" To her surprise, I informed her that she had failed, for talking too much while on the test. The rule states that one should only answer questions put by the examiner while taking the test. Of course, her sergeant husband was very pleased that she had failed the test for he didn't want her driving his new car anyway. After then she seldom talked when we were together and not at all when she took the test again the next week, she passed with flying colors. She nevertheless, dubbed me the "Iron man" who doesn't know you once you walked into my office or on the road test even while being a friend to all, and once I got off work would even hang out with the rest of the boys.

As time moved on, our motor pool commander, Chief Warrant Officer W.A. Bing's tour came to an end. An American of German decent whose last name was Kloozer, who like Mr. Bing, was a Chief Warrant Officer, replaced him. Mr. Kloozer, from day one, seemed to have been bent on trying to prove my incompetence for the position that I held. He was always at odds with the noncommissioned officer in charge of our operation. But since he knew that I did most of the training, testing and record keeping, he was always trying to find something that we were not doing just right. For instance, he came into my office during a training-testing session one day after seeing some of the wives of soldiers sitting before me with their skirts slightly raised or somewhat shorter than they should have been, he suggested that I should arrange the seating so that their backs would be toward my desk. I informed him that I could not administer the test and watch them at the same time with their backs toward me. He then concluded that they could continue sitting facing me.

Then there was another time when he called for me to come over to his office. When I arrived, he said to me, "Specialist Muse, I got you now, and you have no way out this time. I received a report that you had a truckload of soldiers down town Baleduke, some forty miles from post, during the height of the rush hour traffic. Is that correct?" I told him that that was correct. He then asked me "Just how can you justify taking a truck load of trainees down town to train in that kind of situation, when you have so much land on this post and miles and miles of roads stretching some forty or fifty miles through-out this Ammunition depot?" I then pulled out a recently signed copy of the driver's license, which we issued persons who successfully passed the test. I asked him "whose name is signed on it, giving them authority to drive a motor vehicle in France?" He sheepishly replied, "Mine." I then asked him to name any restrictions that may have been indicated on the license. He replied, "There are none." I then asked him if he felt comfortable signing a license for troops that had only been trained and tested on post but who was also authorized to drive down town Bar-le-duke or Paris or anywhere in Europe? He then said to me, "Damn it, Muse, You have won again. Get the hell out of my office."

Several weeks later, Specialist Five, Leon Dewson, my immediate supervisor and noncommissioned officer in charge, went to Paris on a three week pass, leaving me completely in charge of the Driver' Testing operation. Of course, this was no cause for concern to me since I had been doing just about all of the work related to that office anyway. Day after day, he would harshly order me to do both my work as well as his. The most work that he ever did was to go over to the Motor Officer's office, either complaining or answering to some complaint that had been brought against him by someone on the post.

By the end of his second week on leave, The Motor Sergeant called from the Motor Officer's office and said that he was just checking to see if our office was open since he had not heard a squeak from us since Specialist Dewson had been on leave. He then informed me that he was coming over to visit with me right away. He was an older Master Sergeant with mingle brown and grey hair and bluish-grey eyes, whose home was somewhere in the state of Mississippi. Msgt. Gary was obviously a very dedicated career soldier who spent every day as if he was on the battlefield and quite comfortably sported a "take no prisoners" attitude whenever he walked about the compound.

Upon his arrival at my office, he politely greeted me and went straight to the point as to why he had come. He told me that Chief Warrant Officer Kloozer had some concern as to why he hadn't heard a word from our office since Specialist Dawson had been on leave, and that Kloozer had sent him over to see just what was going on. He first wanted to see the ledger of the training sessions, after checking it thoroughly; he then went to the filing cabinet to check the records on file. He carefully scrutinized the freshly waxed and buffed shining floor. He then said, "You have been doing this work all the time, haven't you?' Well I'll be damned if I am going to let Dawson come back in here and mess things up again. When he gets back tell him to report to our office immediately.' In the meantime, find yourself another soldier to assist you and your secretary with this work", he said. He then, just as suddenly as he had come, got up and left, leaving me with the unpleasant task of dealing with a furious ex-supervisor upon his return a few anxious days later.

As scheduled, Specialist Dewson returned all rested and beaming with fond memories of the things that he had seen and experienced in Paris. He started sharing this with me right after he had asked, "Moose (what he called me in mispronouncing my name) how did things go?" I then reluctantly gave him the message that Sergeant Gary had left for him. He wanted to know from me just what he wanted with him. I told him that I didn't know, sparing myself of a possible confrontation with him. He immediately left for the Motor Officer's office. After about an hour or so he returned angry and infuriated, as I knew he would be, while accusing me of knowing why they wanted to see him all the time. As he cleared his desk and file drawers of piles and piles of cups and dishes that he had stored there over the months, he said to me, "I should have known better than to trust a damn preacher after all these years, having been married three times and each time a damn preacher took my wife. And now the best job that I ever had since being in this man's army was just taken from me by you. Of course, this was one of the few times that I resented being called a "preacher". I also would come to feel a bit sorry for him, as he would be assigned to the company's quarters as a maintenance supervisor for the remainder of his duration there on that post.

Maybe I shouldn't have been so hard on myself for I was only resigned and committed to do the work that I was assigned to do, and to do it to the very best of my ability. Never the less, I still had some misgivings as to how things turned out for my ex-supervisor who had spent so much time in the army compared to my entire tour which would be only two years at the most. But again, that was another undeniable evidence that the Lord Our Heavenly Father was forever looking out for me, as undeserving as I may have been.

In the meanwhile, I chose a young specialist 4th class, Lemonel Williams, whose hometown was Modesto, California to assist my secretary and me with the testing and teaching assignments of our office. Specialist Williams was a recent college graduate, with a degree if Psycho Semantics, and professed to be somewhat an aspiring author having produced his first unpublished book titled, of which I aided him by reading the proof, and was convinced that he was indeed a very promising writer. The three of us became quite a team as we worked together on this very tedious job, and we remained the same throughout the rest of our tour of duty there. I felt for sure that we would remain friends for a long long time even after we returned home to the states.

While my military career had just about fallen in place, our marriage was rapidly becoming unglued. The glimmer and sparkle that we once shared while we were back home were becoming more tarnished every day. The tension of being together was becoming so great that I found myself looking forward to the time for Lottie to return home. But the fact that she would be taking with her our daughter Linda, created a dilemma that was most unbearable, for she was the only bright spot left between us. The fact that she would be going back to Cincinnati, to live with her mother until I returned, afforded me no comfort at all. I was not convinced that our problems did not begin while she lived there prior to her coming over to France. At any rate, I continued making plans for their departure as time, at a snail's pace, slowly crept away.

The Saga of the Muses

The awful day finally came. We loaded the car that I had hired to take us to Orly Airport in Paris, the port from which they were to depart. Unknowingly to me at the time, our daughter, Linda, had developed a mild case of the "Mumps." As I attempted to kiss her goodbye, she puckered her little lips and instead of kissing her on the cheek as I had intended, she turned her face and kissed me smack on my lips. With that of course, within a day or so, I too contracted a case of the mumps, which caused the doctor to confine me to quarters for about a week. This confinement was the greatest single aid in helping me to adjust to the sorrow of their departure, and it also provided a reasonable excuse for my red and blurry eyes as I returned to work more than a week later.

Having moved back on post in preparation for our departure, the time was rapidly coming to an end. My replacement had already arrived to be trained for my job. My secretary, who had always been very comical and not too serious when we were together, was suddenly beginning to warm up to me as she expressed her sadness over our having to part company. And for the first time ever, she intimated to my replacement that she would like to give me a goodbye kiss sometime before the final day came. Of course the time came before I had a chance to oblige her in this regard. And the fact that I knew that she was married to a French soldier of German descent, who was serving with the French army in Algiers at the time, didn't help the matter at all. I felt that she was far too desperate to be involved in casual kissing. So I just let her be.

On the morning of our departure, after we had cleared the post, we boarded a convoy of several large twin-coach army busses to La Harve, France, the port from which we were to sail for home. Needless to say, the fact that we were to travel by ship caused me great concern after having heard all the horror stories told by the company of troops when they first arrived by boat some eighteen months earlier. I think that I became seasick just thinking about it. And above all, I found myself wishing for those kind and sympathetic sergeants and officers who had befriended me when I first came into the army and especially those who arranged for me to fly over rather than come by ship when I came over almost two years ago.

Reflections: Trios Fountaines Tour and Beyond

As our convoy snaked its way over the busily traveled highway toward La Havre, once again I found myself reflecting on the experiences that I had during the past eighteen months that I served in France. For instance, I thought on the delightful task that I had in teaching the Sunday morning Bible class at the local educational facilities. All the Protestants churchgoers, including the Post commander and his assistant along with other enlisted men and their dependants stationed on the post, attended these classes.

These classes met while the Catholics were using the chapel for their morning mass. Our Worship services would be held around eleven or twelve after their mass ended. I was indeed quite flattered when any number of high raking officers and their wives approached me about remaining in the educational building for worship services rather than go to the chapel to hear the protestant chaplain preach, which they said meant more to them for they were very serious about their Sunday Morning Worship service. Of course, I felt that it would have been religious treason for me to do so; therefore we always dismissed class in time for us to reassemble at the chapel in spite of the boring sermons that the chaplain may have preached time and time again.

I then thought of the part time job that I worked as bartender at the Officer's Club in Bar-le-duke, which I worked every weekends, holidays and even sometimes on Wednesday nights. I accepted this job, which was offered to me by a fellow soldier and friend of mine. He knew that I needed to supplement my E-4 paycheck in order to support my family who living on the local economy there in Revigny, could barely get by. For this position I drew lots of curious questions and comments from the various officers who were aware that I was an ordained Baptist minister. They related their different stories about someone they knew or had known as a preacher, for one officer the story was about his father, for others someone else that they had known. Who would have thought that to handle liquor, in any way, was religious taboo, and for a minister to serve as bartender was tantamount to an unforgivable sin. My response to them was that I didn't drink but that I had no problem serving them if they were gullible enough to drink, in order for me to acquire the necessary funds that I needed I therefore, gladly served them without any feeling of guilt at all.

Then came the post chaplain to the bar and apologetically ordered a drink, stating that he didn't feel just right having his favorite Bible teacher serving him highballs. After I assured him that it didn't matter to me and that it wouldn't affect our relationship at all, he ambled back to his table and commenced to dance the night away with his guest and others attending the club with him. However after that

I thought that I had figured out just why his sermons seemed to have missed the mark with so many people on our post.

Next to come to the bar was the post Adjutant General, the Major who was censured by the Colonel from Verdun very early in my assignment at Driver's Testing. Time after time he would come up and order a drink without caring to look me in the eyes but making it very obvious that he had not forgotten our unpleasant encounter many months earlier. But as the colonel had promised, he never even spoke to me again. Drink after drink he would order and then slink back to his guest seated at the table with him.

For the remaining time in route I found myself thinking on my rapidly deteriorating marriage and wondering just how would it be when the family and I were together once I reached home and Lottie, and Linda, would have come home after spending so much time with her mother in Cincinnati. Somehow, I was not very optimistic that things would get any better for I was thoroughly convinced that I was not her mother's favorite cup of tea. Therefore I expected her to have continued her effort to pull us apart, that they might remain in Cincinnati.

By now we were making our initial approach to the port of La Havre. As wide-open countryside gave way to small sparsely inhabited townships, which became more thickly populated with every mile we traveled. Then it was very obvious that we were in the center of a bustling metropolis, the city of Le' Havre, France. Weaving through the very busy streets, our convoy finally roared to a stop at the seaside, with noisy seagulls soaring overhead as if they were anxiously welcoming us to port, and where our ship, the USS Randall, was waiting for what was to be it's final voyage before being scrapped, to ferry us back home to the good ole United States of America. We went directly from our busses onto the ship. By the time we had finished dinner in the ship's musty old mess hall where we all ate like pigs before retiring to our cramped berths as we waited for our departure. By then night had befallen us. Soon thereafter, we heard a few loud blasts from the ship's wailing and mournful fog hog horn and felt a sharp jerk, and knew without a doubt, that we were on our way home at last.

The first leg of our voyage took us by way of the English Channel, where we were to pick up additional passengers and cargo in England sometime during the night. When daylight came we had made our stop and were already on the high sea headed for the New York harbor, which we were to reach some nine days later.

Day after day, all that we saw from the fog-shrouded ship were the unending mist that enveloped the ship, breaking and billowing waves foaming on the liquid horizon far away from us, and great schools of porpoises leaping beside and in the wake of the ship. Sometimes there were as many as fifty to a hundred successively leaping in and out of the water with such precision as if they were performing some acrobatic stunts for the soldiers lounging on its heaving deck. The soldiers all seemed to have been greatly fascinated by all these occurrences. But as for me, I was so seasick that I could barely raise my head, and that was not without me throwing up all over the deck. Throughout the entire voyage the most food that I ate were roasted salty peanuts constantly fed to me by my trusty friend and former co-worker, Private Williams, who convinced me that unless I at least ate something, that I would end up in the sick bay for the duration of our travel.

Finally, on the ninth day we found ourselves anchored just off the shores of New York Harbor, where we were to remain on board until the next day. For we had arrived within the view of the Statue of Liberty, with its outstretched arm and flaming torch, on the first Monday of September which of course, was Labor Day, a national holiday, and no one was working to process us off the ship and out of the army. We had to just sit and watch all the festival celebrations going on across the harbor from the ship which had been our home of torture for almost two whole weeks by now. We were so close and yet so far away from being set free to go back to our homes and families again.

Very early on Tuesday morning, we were mustered off the ship and ferried over to Fort Hamilton, New York, where we were immediately processed out of military service. We loaded on different busses for our different destinations and just like that, the most trying two years of my life unbelievably came to an end. Thereby yielding me an experience of mixed opinions, one that I wouldn't trade for a million dollars, and for which I would not give one nickel to repeat. But I was however, ever so thankful that my entire two years in military service was served during a time of peace, without our nation being in any combative conflict with any other nation or country.

On the bus I couldn't help but notice, that while we soldiers, blacks and whites sat together just as we had done for the past two years. But as we neared the state of Alabama, the white soldiers, without announcing it, quietly got up and ambled toward the front of the bus, leaving the few black soldiers seated throughout the bus, mostly in small knots of puzzled and frustrated humanity. Therefore, bringing afresh to mind the stalk reality that we were to face, even from them, as we all returned home and to a "business as usual" southland to which we were anxiously returning. Even though in Montgomery the city busses had been desegregated since December 1956 and this was September 1960, this left me to conclude that indeed "the more things change, the more they remain the same."

Interstate transportation however, would become desegregated a few years later and that would not be without terrible violent attacks and bloody beatings of the heroic "Freedom Riders" blacks and whites, men and women, from several northern and eastern cities across this nation, who would put their lives on the line in the face of great danger of senseless mobs of un-godly men to achieve this right on all our behalf, blacks and whites alike.

Whatever the case, I returned home from the army with a stronger than ever resolve to join in the fight for equality and first class citizenship for my self, my family and for people of all races and culture. For this world belongs only to Him who created both it and us as well. I felt that the most effective method of doing this was to impact the lives of leaders of the Black community, namely the pastors of the various churches and denominations. Therefore going to school and teaching in the seminary were to be my first step in this direction. My next step would come years later in the founding of a Bible Institute and Theological Center that would be committed to both this liberating and developmental philosophy, as well as to the promotion of Christian principles and practices.

97. My basic training photo.

Chapter 12

Resuming Life after My Military Tour of Duty
(1960 – 1966)

The excitement of being back home was short lived as reality set in. First, I had to find a place to live, for the wife and I had given up our apartment and she had moved in with her grandparents upon my induction. And they had decided to move to Cincinnati while I was in service, after placing such furniture that we had in storage. I therefore went to my mother's house, which was far too crowded with all the children for me. Furthermore, I readily realized that, while they had made great advancements since I had been gone; there was an obvious need that whatever help my meager income would offer could make things better for them. I thought, therefore, that instead of moving into an apartment of my own, if we could find a house large enough to accommodate us all we could pool our resources and together raise our standard of living. After relating this to the wife, who was still in Cincinnati, she readily agreed that if I found a large enough house for them, and us she would gladly move back in with us.

After searching for a week or more, I finally found a large white house on Cleveland Avenue that seemed to be just the place we needed. So once more we moved in and set up house while I awaited the return of the wife and baby who would come after remaining with her mother in Cincinnati some two more weeks. Once again there was much happiness and joy of being with the family again.

Then there was the matter of returning to work on the job that I had before going into the army. According to law, employers were compelled to rehire employees who worked for them before being inducted into service. And of course, my former employer honored this demand; however, there were some white women with whom I had worked prior, who had risen to manager and other positions who did not welcome me back. They accused me of being mean and brashy toward them and said that I felt that I didn't have to listen to them as they gave me orders. Of course this was the lie they told in the attempt to get the boss to let me go. The manager's husband was doing the work that I had previously done before going into service. After we had a private conference between the two of us, Mr. Sullivan, with tears in his eyes, told me that it would probably be best if I sought employment elsewhere; because they would always be picking on me for one reason or the other. He said that he would call Mr. Kahn, a co-owner of the Sunday Dinner Produce Company, to see if he would hire me there. Of course, Mr. Kahn and I had been friends since we first met while he doubled as salesman for the company, and I was the ordering clerk at Sully's. He became so impressed with my business acumen until he told me that I shouldn't be working for anyone but myself. With that he informed me that if I found a suitable location that he would build me a restaurant and set it up for me without any cost to myself. He said that all that he would want me to do was to use my skills in operating the business. However, before this transaction could take place, I was drafted into the army. In the meantime, he and Mr. Sullivan had ventured into a similar project, which proved a sheer disaster. It had begun and folded up long before I got out of the service.

Mr. Kahn and I arranged to meet a few days later. After greeting me rather warmly and asking me about my military experiences, he related to me the experience that he and Mr. Sullivan had had in their joint venture, and that he was not as enthusiastic about going into this kind of business as before. However, he said that if I found a building in a suitable location, he would still help me to get set up and would support me until I got on my feet in it. In the meanwhile, he said that since I needed work now, that he would introduce me to the warehouse manager and recommend that I be the first available job that he would have come open. Of course, I didn't have to be a Harvard graduate to recognize the resentment on the manager's face as the boss had personally brought me to him and made such recommendation. Never the less, he promised him that he would comply. But deep in our hearts we both knew that he had no intention of doing so.

After waiting for more than a week without hearing anything from the warehouse manager, I once again went by to see Mr. Kahn. He seemed to have been somewhat disturbed in that I had not been hired. He informed me that the only person that they hired was the Warehouse

Manager, and that they didn't interfere with the way that he operated the business as long as he satisfactorily ran it, and in case that he didn't they would release him of that responsibility. "However," he said, "Usually we expect him to take our personal recommendations seriously, which apparently he hasn't, for I know that a white boy left about a week ago and his job should still be open." Having said this, he invited me to accompany him to the manager's office, where upon he inquired about the job that the man had left and why he had not offered that job to me. He also informed him that he was not interested in saving a particular job for a white man when he thought that I was just as qualified to do it. After this I was immediately hired, despite much resentment by the manager. I never became one of his favorite employees the whole time that I was employed there.

Once hired, I recognized just why this job was reserved for a white person. For it was driving a refrigerated frozen food truck delivering small cases of frozen foods to public schools and restaurants around the city. This was by far easier than loading groceries in the warehouse some of which weighed as much as a hundred pounds. That job was reserved only for the black men to perform. All the time the manager taunted me and showed his resentment for me especially when other white people were around, as long as I remained on that job.

I was only relieved of this condition when I was commissioned as Missionary by the American Sunday School Union, an age-old Christian organization headquartered in Philadelphia, Pennsylvania, which played a prominent role in the religious life of early pioneers as they traveled by covered wagon on their westward movement during the early years of this nation. Among the missionaries of whom they boasted was the noted Daniel Webster, who became famous for his great English dictionary which is still of great use to us today.

I was to serve a several-county area in south and southeastern Alabama, organizing Sunday Schools, conducting Vacation Bibles Schools, distributing clothing, (new and used) and providing money and food for poverty-stricken people in the rural areas of my district. We also distributed a very fine line of Sunday school commentaries, Vacation Bible School publications and other religious materials to churches in these areas. This company produced the very finest of such materials. I embarked upon a mission that was most fulfilling and a way of life that would alter and dominate the rest of my life. I would remain in this position for the next seven years and it would over lap the tenure of my first pastorate, which was the First Baptist Church of Prattville, Alabama. This position of pastor I would also hold for seven years. They would prove to be most meaningful years of all times to me. I would develop a love for these members that would always be unmatched regardless to where I may be privileged to serve.

While pastoring in Prattville, our marriage continued to unravel. This irreparable erosion was expressed in uncontrollable outbursts of verbal abuse and physical violence that was mostly initiated by the wife. It seemed that she was never satisfied once she came home from Cincinnati, even after we moved out to our own apartment away from the rest of the family. This continued time and time again, until her grandmother came to take her back to Cincinnati about the third year of my pastorate in Prattville. She came under the pretense of coming to see if she could help in the mending of our broken relationship. But her

141

husband sent me word that she had come, despite his protest, to break us up.

Of course this was very devastating to me and I came down with a serious case of bleeding ulcers and a nervous condition that led me to think that I would lose my mind. Not because I wanted her to stay with me when she wanted so badly to leave. But it was because our five-year-old daughter, Linda, had become my heart, the object of my affection and the very reason for me to live. Therefore, taking her away was the most unbearable experience that I had ever known, and one of which I almost didn't survive. But, survive I must, and survive I did. That's the reason I am here to write this account today and to do the many things that I have been privileged to do since that time. I finally gave up on the possibility of reconciliation after my mother-in-law advised me not to ever call her house again. I then informed the church that the breakup was final. At that time I realized that our marriage was over after seven years of blissful, joyful and finally of many tormenting experiences, leaving scars in my heart of which there is no healing.

Pulling my life together after our devastating breakup was a very difficult task at best for me. First, I had to deal with very serious physical and emotional health problems. Then there was the matter of dealing with the church as an unmarried pastor. However, to my surprise, they were far more sympathetic with me than I ever thought they would be. Finally, there was an aching need for me to find a reliable companion to aid me in dealing with my personal and social life. I needed help to bring about healing for my physical, emotional and spiritual needs. This latter need was met as I started eyeing a young but very mature young school teacher who served as musician for the church. She was also in the process of recovering from a very abusive and tormenting marriage of her own to a very popular and able older minister. He, despite his extraordinary preaching ability, was possessed with an uncontrollable problem with alcohol and or drugs. This resulted in her having shattered nerves and debilitating emotional and physical stresses. The situation had resulted in their permanent breakup and ultimately their divorce, leaving her with a small very bright young son, "Michael", He was about five years old at this time, and her entire life revolved around him.

Little did I know at the time that this would form the nucleolus of my family for the rest of my life, (at least for the next forty-five years as of the time of this writing) After a brief but serious courtship Mamie and I were married and blessed with a precious little daughter, whom we named "Valerie", because that name signified "Strength" and was a sort of an adopted code name that I had given her mother long before she came along, for at that time my life's situation was crying for strong shoulders to lean on and she offered such shoulders to me.

After much discussion and consideration as the affect that our getting married would have on the church, for I was aware of the many churches that have been devastated by their pastor getting a divorce, and many of those who survived this first phase could not tolerate him marrying the second time, and especially to a member of the flock. Having considered all the possible ins and outs relating to this matter, we finally decided that the pluses by far out weighted the minuses and that even if worse came to worse, and the church would not accept us that we would move on and resume a pastorate elsewhere. So we decided to become secretly married on St. Patrick's Day, and to make it known at a designated time in the near future. In the meantime we would be having our house built in an upscale suburban community some sixteen miles east of Montgomery. We decided that we would announce both our marriage and the building of the house at the same time.

The designated time finally came; the time had come when we would make known our marriage to the church. That Sunday morning after nervously preaching the sermon, I informed them that I had a special announcement to make. Of course, one could but feel the tension of anticipation and suspicion as they sat stoically silent waiting to see just what I had to say. I then commenced to inform them, by telling them that while I knew the possible devastating effect that our marriage could have on the church and that they might see fit to relieve me as pastor, for which I would humbly apologize; but that I was also conscious of the many churches across the nation who would not have a pastor unless he was married. I concluded by telling them that what ever their reaction would be, that we were married and that we would remain thus without any hard feeling from us toward them should they decide to relieve me of my pastoral responsibility.

There was no applause or outburst of sighs of happiness or disappointment. There was only a few stretched moments of eerie silence with member glancing first at one another and then toward the platform where I nervously stood, leaving me feeling that I stood before as many seats of judgment as there were members present at that time, as I anxiously awaited their unpredictable verdict.

Finally, the silence was broken by the noble and authoritative voice of an old lady, sister Lula Underwood, who could have rightly been considered "Mother of the church" since she was held in such high esteem and greatly respected by the majority of the membership. Although she was an older woman, she ranked very highly among the most educated members, being a long since retired teacher of the Autauga County Public Schools system. She was also president of the Missionary Society of the church, and could have been considered the "unappointed" leader of the women of our church. Her frequently quoted advice to me always was "Reverend Muse, Stand on your feet, and be a man." Today, she breaks the eerie silence saying, "Ladies, I don't know if you heard what I just heard. I heard our pastor say that he has chosen a wife from among us. I don't know if you understand just what that means. As I have always told you, 'our pastor will not be here with us very long. For the Lord will take him far from here and will lift him to an even greater height than we can ever become or support.' This means that wherever he goes, one of us will be with him and by his side. Therefore I would like to place in motion, that the women of this church embrace this marriage and that we will all stand on our feet as a gesture of blessing and congratulation to the pastor and his newly taken bride. And that we will honor them with a special wedding shower with in the next three weeks."

The chairman of Deacons rose to carry the motion, he prefaced it by stating, "As chairman of the Board of deacons, I would like that this entire church, both men and women, boys and girls make this gesture unanimous, and that we will join the women in showering them on the designated day as chosen by the church." With this we were relieved of a mountainous burden and from then on enjoyed the rest of our tenure there not only as the family of God, but as a family among many, both in the church and throughout the church, the community and the city at large. Three weeks later they gave us a wedding shower, giving us so many gifts that they filled both of our cars,

passenger compartments and trunks as well. Most of which
came in very handy as we moved into our newly built house
around the same time and we just about needed everything
that they gave to us.

Although the church accepted our marriage without even
a shade of reservation, and even though through this
marriage I gained one of the finest Mothers-in-law that any
son or daughter could ever hope for. Regretfully, the same
could not be said of my new Father-in-law, who was a
thousand times just the opposite of what she was. He
violently hated me from the very beginning and would
continue to do so until his dying day some twenty years
later, without even allowing me a chance to prove to him
that I would be the best husband that his daughter could
ever possibly find anywhere. His resentment toward me
was so strong that he barred me from his home and would
not even allow me to visit his wife, my Mother-in-law even
after she returned home from a serious stomach surgery
and insisted that I would come to visit her. Obliging her
request, I did visit her once she was home only to have her
send me word not to come back again as he had so hatefully
demanded her to do. I was even informed by a white
insurance agent that he kept his shotgun loaded and was
publishing the fact that he intended to shoot me if I ever
darkened his door again. He even disinherited my wife so
that she would have no part in his very megar estate, which
would be divided among his children after his death and
the death of their mother, which to say the least, was not
worth enough for him to have gone to the trouble to draw
up the papers, but enough however, for him to show how
strongly he resented our being married.

When he died I had been away all week in revival at our
church in Auburn. (For I had been extended and accepted

the call to the pastorate there about four years after our marriage) and I had scheduled a wedding on the Saturday of the funeral, but my dear Mother-in-law wanted so badly for me to come to the funeral, that she changed the hour of the service to a much later hour than they had previously planned to allow me enough time to get there. Even so, I arrived somewhat late and the funeral had already begun when I got there. The wedding party had arrived late for the wedding that I was to perform and I just couldn't get away on time. Therefore making me late for the funeral even after I drove far above the speed limit the entire sixty-five miles from Auburn to Prattville, in the effort to make up for the lost time. For the family's sake I was delighted to offer such comfort as my humble presence had been requested. But still I was somewhat saddened that our relationship could not have been different and thereby causing less stress on our children and the rest of his family who loved and respected him so dearly.

Well, having moved into our new home, the four of us settled in, and in the process of becoming a family we enjoyed many years of joyful experiences. For the two of us, Mamie and I, watching the children grow up was indeed a most rewarding experience. Each day was filled with excitements as we watched them experience their first snow, which was quite a rarity in this part of the country. But, from time to time it came as a surprise to us all. We observed their excitement as they watched the wild squirrels and rabbits that frequently and playfully roamed across our lawn. They ignored our frisky little dog "Skipper" which we sometimes tied on a lease near the garden spot to keep them away. We came home from church on several occasions and would find them, dog, rabbit and squirrels playing together. We finally gave up on them, letting the dog and other varmints roam both yard and garden unbothered.

We had an occasion to laugh at Michael one day when he seemed to have taken wings, leaving both shoes flying over his head while running from a snake that he saw in the tall grass on a vacant lot across the street in front of the house. We used the lot as a garden before it was sold and a house was built on it. Sometimes we would go biking on one of the several country roads that surrounded our suburban home. At times the four of us would go fishing in some over-grown pond that I once knew as a fairly good fishing hole. Most times we caught only a few small breams, which to them, were "whoppers". They insisted on cooking and eating them no matter how small they were

There are many laughable and enjoyable memories resulting from watching the children grow up and listening to their innocent conversations about incidents and experiences that they had, Michael, for instance, always dreamed of doing manly things such as, becoming a fireman, then a policeman, then a cowboy, then a soldier and getting married. But he never mentioned, even once, that he wished to become a preacher and pastor, which he has successfully done for a number of churches over the years. At this time he even pastors the historical Dexter Avenue Baptist Church of Montgomery, Alabama, which was made famous as the church pastored by the late Reverend Doctor Martin Luther King Jr. while he led the civil rights movements during the turbulent years of the mid fifties and early sixties.

Valerie, on the other hand, even as a very small child, loved flowers and particularly, the blooming crimson clover that produced a bright fuzzy velvet-colored blossom. It grew in abundance along the incomplete super highway that at that time ended just beyond the exit to our new home. At three years of age, on the days that I would keep her while her mother went to work, she would demand that I take her picture posing as a model among the clover. Even today, when she and her family come home to visit when the clover is in bloom, she always bring me a few blooming pods, letting me know just how meaningful those precious moments were to her.

However, the incident that merited the loudest laugh happened one night after she got a splinter in her foot. She told her mother about it, and she sent her to me to get it out. I told her to bring me a razorblade, a needle and a pair of tweezers. She then crawled upon my lap and stretched her skinny little leg forward with her splinter pierced foot near my face. I then took the razorblade and trimmed the tough outer skin away; then I took the needle and gently pricked the splinter to the surface. Finally I plucked it out with the tweezers. Val was so excited as she searched for words to compliment me for having made her well. She said, "Oh daddy you are a doctor, aren't you?" I answered her, "No Val, I am not a doctor." She thought for a moment and said again, "Daddy, if you are not a doctor, why do they call you doctor at the churches that you go to?" I informed her that it was not uncommon for people at church to call the minister "doctor," but that did not mean that he is one. After a brief pause, she again asked me, "Daddy you are not even a "foot doctor?" I replied, "No Valerie, I am not even a foot doctor." After a much longer pause, she said to me, "Daddy you know something, you ain't nothing." To this, I with an uneasy smirk was compelled to agree.

Her real test of fate however, came one Sunday morning when she was five years of age. Sunday after Sunday we had driven across the bridge over the highway and turned left on the freeway to Prattville where I had pastored for the past seven years. That Sunday morning instead of crossing the bridge, I turned right and headed in the opposite direction. Valerie standing between her mother and me asked "Daddy, you are not going to Prattville today?" Trying not to be perturbed I answer "No Val I am not going to Prattville today." She then asked, "Daddy are you going to get a new church?" Trying to remain polite I said to her, "Valerie, I don't know, all I know is that I will be preaching at a new church today." By then her mother told her to stop bothering me for I needed to think as I drove the car. ...After a lengthy pause, she says to me, "Daddy if you want that church, I will tell you how to get it." I asked her "How?" She said, "Don't preach too loud and don't preach too long." After she said that she kept silent as she stood between her mother and me the rest of the way to the church.

As I stood to preach that morning, I introduced the family and had Valerie to remain standing after Mamie and Michael had sat. Then I told the church what she had told me as to how to get the church, which they found to be amusingly true. A year later when they commenced to call a pastor, strangely enough, they couldn't remember what I preached about, neither could they remember how I looked, nor could they even remember my name nor the church that I pastored. They only remembered the preacher that had the little girl who told him "Don't preach too loud and don't preach too long." She is now a full grown woman with a family of her own, but she still reminds me after thirty six years of pastoring that church, that she got it for me, which I cannot truthfully deny.

Our house served as a haven of rest and adventure for all of us. Its location sixteen miles east of Montgomery provided just the right atmosphere that I needed, having been born and raised on the farm. The rest of the family found it to be rather enchanting to them as well. It was nestled on a large tree covered plot amidst tall murmuring pines and a few sweet gum and oak trees. Many of them, at that time, were no taller than shrubbery or as some would call them, "undergrowth." But they would become a dangerous menace in future years, especially the pines, growing in heights of one hundred to a hundred and fifty or more feet tall. And first, one by one, they would fall from time to time, either blown down by occasional wind storms or dying from being affected by hordes of pine beetles that sought out any pine whose bark was skinned in the slightest way. Some fell on the yard and others on the house. We finally had them all removed for the safety of the house and family.

A babbling brook zigzagged between our property and that of our neighbors, whose back yards joined ours. It always had water in it except during the driest part of the summer months. It served a property mark in the edge of the dense woods behind our house. It made a perfect sanctuary for the wild animals that were no stranger at our back yard patio door. There were squirrels, rabbits, opossums, raccoons, and even sometimes, unwanted snakes that shared our yard with us.

We were just far enough from the Interstate highway to hear the rumble of traffic and the faint sound of sirens of emergency vehicles as they rushed to the scene of some accident on the busy freeway without being terribly discomforted by the noise thereon. This distance, far enough from the city would also prove to be a great advantage to us. It gave us easy access to travel to the church in the city of Auburn, some forty miles from where we live. This humble setting would indeed provide for our family a haven of growth, development, and life for untold years. Even today Although the children have married and moved out with their own families, Mamie and I have no intention to move elsewhere, no, not even into the rather luxurious parsonage that was built for us some years ago next to the church which I have pastored for almost forty years.

#8. The family group.
Wanda, Michael, Valerie and myself

Chapter 13

College Experience at Selma University (1967 – 1985)

Everything having pretty well fallen into place, I began thinking about resuming my studies in preparation for the Christian ministry. I had always dreamed of attending our local Baptist school, Selma University, a small religious school sponsored by the "Black" Alabama Baptist State Convention, and like the name implies, the school is located in Selma, Alabama. And is one of the few Historical Black Colleges and Universities, (HBCU) located in the state. Selma University is famous for training many of the leading Baptist pastors of black churches from coast to coast across this nation. A degree from there was coveted by many more who for some reason may not have found it possible to study there, but continue to look for a time when the opportunity might arise.

In the not-too-distant past, Selma University served as a sort of "catch-all" for Blacks throughout the "Black Belt" area, (so called because of the rich dark-colored soil which stretches across this wide area of south central and southwest Alabama, and is very conducive for the growing of many of the native crops, such as cotton, corn and other such crops as needed for food for humans and animals.) If our people desired an education from high school through the college level, they most likely would attend Selma University. This was largely due because of the segregated south in which it was located, but also because of its affordability so far as tuition was concerned. And the quality of education there was comparable to that of any school of its size that served our people anywhere in the southern United States, therefore creating strong competition between other black institutions of higher learning contending for its graduates who wished to further study for higher degrees. For this reason I had no hesitation in falsely dropping its name when ever I had been asked where I had attended seminary when I was in the army. Since I was quite well read I could pretty well exceed the expectation of those who inquired, and since most of them had no earthly idea as to what a theological study involved. And my responsibility in that department was strictly as a volunteer at any rate; no further proof of my enrollment was needed or required.

But now the time had come for me to realize my greatest dream, I would become a student at Selma University. My first enrollment came just before the break-up my first marriage. I would work at night and drive the fifty miles from Montgomery to Selma and attend classes all-day and back to Montgomery for work at night. Most days I shared a ride with two other ministerial students, one who also worked nights. The other was a full time pastor of a church in Montgomery. Of course, this very strenuous schedule was more than I could endure, I became most worn and exhausted before the end of the second semester, and going to the doctor, he wouldn't even allow me to go back home, but sent me straight from his office to the hospital, where I remained long enough to lose the second semester credits for that year. Of course, I dropped out for that year, only to return several years later with the insatiable determination to ride it through come what may.

Several years into my second marriage, the next opportunity came for me to enter college. I no longer worked nights, and the government had just passed a new GI bill which would grant me one month of education for each month that I had spent in the army, plus a full month for each quarter of a month. Since I had spent twenty-four months and a few days therein, I was entitled to a total of twenty-five months of education. This along with the small salary from the church I was able to enroll with some assurance of being able to complete the course requirement for the Bachelor's degree in Theology.

By the time that I had finished these twenty five months, President Lyndon Johnson increased the allocation for veterans to forty eight months giving me more than enough support to finish the pursued degree with some extra finance for tuitions well toward the second degree from the Alabama State University, which I acquired several years later.

Upon entering the classroom for the first time in six years after my high school graduation, at first I felt a bit intimidated having to study with students so young who had so recently graduated from high school. However, my intimidation was short lived as teachers put certain questions before us, and after seeing that most of them, didn't have the slightest answer, they either called on me for the answer or recognized my raised hand and allowed me to answer them.

Very soon while attending classes, I found myself conscientiously on guard against being seen as an "old nerd" or a show-off by the rest of the students with whom I studied. But I realized that I hadn't been completely successful in this effort as I walked alone across the campus one day. As I approached two young men who were non-ministerial students (as most of the students in attendance were,) who were slightly older than most other students attending Selma University, as they stood near the back of a parked car on the lot, when one of them remarked to the other, "You see that S.O.B. coming there?" "Man, that's a smart M.F." The other one answered, "You mean the Reverend?" He said, "Yes, that S.O.B. knows everything. The teachers always call on him whenever no one else can answer, and he always knows the answer." Of course, I was not supposed to have heard them, and if so I should have been terribly offended, and should have become angry at the least. So I pretended not to have heard them, for even though their choices of words were bad, I felt that they had paid me the highest compliment. Therefore when I was near enough to greet them, I politely said, "I hope you gentlemen are having a nice day, I'll see you in our next class." They both replied almost as one, "Thank you Reverend, I hope you the same." I kept walking pass them as if nothing at all had happened.

My four years study at Selma University, for the most part, moved along rather smoothly. The only problem I had, so far as academics was concerned, was with classes of a mathematics or algebraic nature, It was in this area that I had to rely on some other students for help. We would form small study groups and would often study well into the night several nights each week during the semesters while enrolled in these classes I often helped them with just about all other classes that we were required to take, but seriously needed their help as I undertook to study in these two subjects. In fact, I excelled so well in other subjects that I was assigned to teach several classes as early as my junior year and remained on there teaching in the Religious Department long after I graduated.

At first I taught non-ministerial students Old and New Testaments, as they were required to take these courses in Bible since they were enrolled in a religious institution. I found myself quite fitted for this challenge since I had worked for years as a missionary teaching course in Bible throughout my field of mission, and not because I was smarter than any other student with similar experience. Later I was given the responsibility to teach theological students as well. For the next fifteen years with the exception of some brief interruptions, I would remain on the faculty at this quite well known Historical Black University, for almost twenty years, a position that was coveted by many who were by far more qualified to teach than I was.

My study was dolefully interrupted in April of 1968 by the slaying of Dr. Martin Luther King, who had given so much to make things better for our people and the nation as a whole. His death caused me to renew my determination and commitment to do more toward helping to bring about needed changes to benefit our people in their struggle for social justice and religious reformation.

These years of study at S.U. were indeed the most advantageous years of my academic experience. First there was the constant interchanging with pastors already experienced in the work, but who had returned for refreshers courses or to acquire the degree they had always wanted, but until now were not able to pursue it. Fellowship with these and other theological students can never be adequately evaluated, and have had a lasting impact on my life and work throughout my entire life.

Then there was the study and fellowship with other non-theological students who were eagerly pursuing degrees in many other fields. Some went on to become principals of schools; some teachers; some lawyers, one a medical doctor, and still others became accountants or some other specialized field or vocation. All of whom were drilled with the notion that they were privileged to get an education not just to make money, but that they might better serve our people and somehow help in making our world a better place in which to live.

Chapter 14

The Tragedy on Pleasant Avenue
(1970 - 1980)

During my third year study at Selma things seems to have fallen into place far better than I expected. My classes were most challenging and ministry related, forcing me to study with much more interest than I had done at any time heretofore. The church that I pastored, (The First Baptist church in Prattville, for I had not yet received the call from Ebenezer, Auburn) was pretty much operating without much stress apart from the ever present apathy that was common among the majority of the members. However, since I had resolved that they would not accept any changes that I would have offered them, I therefore just preached to them and, "let them drift" so to speak.

When I returned home from service I readily welcome the news that mother, after these years, had found someone with whom to share her life. His name was Paul. All the children affectionately called him "Mr. Paul." He and mother had known each other for quite some time before they decided to get married. He was very kind and gentler to mom and all the children and accepted all of us as though we were his very own, the older ones as well as the young. In their marriage we saw mother in a state of happiness that she was not known to have experience in the past. In fact, the whole family seemed to settle in around Mr. Paul. And we all loved him very much.

Mr. Paul having assumed full responsibility toward mother and the family, even putting them on his health and accident insurance where he worked as a long distance truck driver, delivering French provincial furniture for a company that made it. He also was very dutiful in all other responsibilities toward them such as paying tuition for those who were in college, leaving me having to assist only on such occasions as when they needed me, thus allowing me the freedom to devote more time to my immediate family and Religious studies at home until such time as I would be able to enroll at Selma University where I would receive a more formal training.

After renting houses in several areas throughout the city, they finally leased a very attractive house on a large tree-covered lot on Pleasant Avenue, which was located not too far from downtown Montgomery. The house was obviously well kept and sported a bright fresh coat of paint, both inside and out. All kind of flowering trees and flowering plants bedecked the large yards front and back, which was recessed just far enough from the street to give it a semi-secluded air to anyone who viewed it from the mildly busy street. Both the house and its surroundings reflected a special pride that the owners had in them before they vacated them and moved from this rapidly transitioning neighborhood as whites moved out and blacks moved in. This was an ideal home for our rather large but dwindling family living there. The spacious lawns afforded the perfect setting for cookouts and out-door weddings and the likes, for at least one of our sibling, Minnie, and husband Clarence, were married on its lawn. Our brother Nelson performed the ceremony. I was contented with just looking on, and wishing them well. Two older sisters, Lucile and Mary Pearl having married earlier, leaving Joe, Ida, Richard and Jimmy still living with Mother and Paul.

In a few months I entered Selma University, I secured an apartment and lived off campus, living there Monday through Thursday, and returning home on Friday mornings, which made studying and fellowship much easier for me as a full-time student. This allowed me to mingle with other ministerial students after classes each day, both those living on and off campus. We usually met at one of the men's dormitories or some other building on campus or at a nearby restaurant just outside the campus gate. There we would spend long after-school hours discussing things that we had studied during the day; or just joking around and light heartily talking about any thing that may cross our minds.

It was during one of these after-school get-togethers during my Junior year, that I received a phone call on a phone from a building across the campus and was summoned to hurry for it was my wife, and that she sounded very seriously concerned about something. Rushing to the telephone, Mamie informed me that Mr. Paul had shot himself earlier during the day. Not knowing what to say, I asked, "Was it an accident?" "Is he in the hospital?" "How is he doing?" She interrupted, "Willie, he is dead, He committed suicide." This news simply floored me and left me for a moment entirely numb and speechless. Moments later after regaining my composure, I thanked her with the few words that I could muster out, and like a zombie ambled mournfully back to share the grotesque news with the group who was anxiously waiting to see just what the phone call was about. Upon being informed, they all reached out to me with heart-felt sympathy and prayers. While I was debating as to whether I should depart immediately for Montgomery, or just call and wait until the next day to join them in their grief. There was so much confusion and grief going on in my mind until I was at a loss as to just what to do.

My hesitation however, was ended when one of the students who pastored a church in the city just outside the gate of the campus said to me, "Muse, you know that your mother needs you at this time. She not only needs you but she is waiting for you, for you are all she has to help her now. Get ready and I will drive you over to Montgomery, and remain with you as long as is necessary." With that, others offered to accompany us but he deemed that only the two of us should go during this intense incident of grief and pain, in order that the family may have some time to work through the grief process as much alone as possible.

When we arrived it was early night, and sure enough Mother and family were eagerly looking for me. Mother's shrill and lamenting screams pervaded the scene upon the first glimpse of my presence at this doleful house of mourning. The other children sat teary-eyed starring with a thousand unasked questions lurking in their aching and confused hearts. After a moment or composure, mother said, "Sonny, I am glad that you finally came, I have been looking for you ever since this happen." She then showed me one of the several letters that Paul had written and placed in conspicuous places about the house, mainly apologizing for his self-destructive action, the hurt that he had caused her, and to eliminate any suspicion that she had in any way, contributed to the cause of his death.

After several hours trying to console mother and the family, the minister who drove me home offered prayer, and we departed on our late night return trip to Selma.

In route, I had plenty of time to think about possible causes as to just why Mr. Paul may have done this awful thing, first to himself, then to our mother and to us. Then I remembered some things that he said to mother and me as I drove them to Orrville a few days earlier to attend the funeral of a very close family friend who had died in his sleep during the night after working in the field all day.

On this trip, Mr. Paul informed us that while he was in the army years ago, he experienced very serious and unbearable headaches that grew progressively worse in time. After a series of exams, doctors had ruled that his headaches were only imaginary and couldn't be treated. He was granted a Medical Discharge, even before he had served enough time to become eligible to receive GI benefits, which would have allowed him to build a house as many of us had done. He indicated that after a while those awful headaches stopped, but now, he said, "they were coming back with increased frequency and that he certainly would not tolerate them again." Even after mother reminded him that he would have no choice if they came back. He still said that he would not tolerate such pain. Having said this, we drove the rest of the way in almost total silence speaking only intermittently to each other all the way to the funeral and back. It all came back to me as I rode along and in my head, searched for answers.

According to mom, the morning of his death started like any normal day. Ida Bell was away attending college at Spelman, in Atlanta. Joe was at Alabama State University, almost within walking distance of Pleasant Avenue. The other brothers, Richard and Jimmy had gone through their usual early morning routines and had already left for school.

But Jimmy, the youngest, said that for some unknown reason he felt uncomfortable and so completely out of place at school that morning, therefore, without even getting the required excuse from the principal's office, he left and returned home. He said that to his surprise, neither Mr. Paul nor mother asked him why he had come back home. He said that Mr. Paul immediately sent him to the store about a block away to pick up something for him. He later realized that this was done only to get him out of the house while he carried out his fatal plan.

He said that as he was returning to the house with whatever items he had purchased at the store, that he heard mom screaming and wailing on the porch as she frantically pointed toward the open door to the inside of the house. Casting the items to the ground, he ran to her side and going into the house he finds Mr. Paul slumped over in the over-size chair which he had carefully covered with a sheet of plastic to protect it from becoming soaked with the blood that profussively spurted from the single bullet wound in his head. The small caliber rifle lay at his feet, and several suicide notes had been conspicuously placed throughout the room. Jimmy then called the police, who after a brief investigation, called the funeral home to pick up the body. In the meantime, Joe was returning home from Alabama State University and seeing all the commotion, ran as fast as he could to the fatal scene.

Of course, the shock and grief were almost too much for us to endure, and yet we had to toughen up and bear it. The funeral was held several days later with many relatives and caring friends in attendance. With that, the most perfect, loving husband and the most caring step-dad and personal friend had come to an end. But his precious memories will always linger in our hearts and mother would cherish his love and memories until her death many years later.

#11. Ebenezer Baptist Church, Auburn Alabama

Chapter 15

"Life Must Go On"

The above title was the title of a sermon that a pastor preached on Sunday morning September 15th 1963. I was worshiping with them on that morning. The service was well under way when the telephone rang for the pastor, the caller insisting that it was very urgent. He excused himself from the pulpit for a few minutes. On his return he informed the church of a tragedy of historical proportion that had taken place. Four little innocent Black girls had just been killed by a bomb planted somewhere in or near the Sunday school area of the Sixteenth Street Baptist church in Birmingham. Amidst strong cries of anguish and sorrow of worshippers, the pastor with a brief explanation, immediately changed the title of his morning sermon. He preached of the subject "Life Must Go On" Needless-to say, the sermon was very suitable for such sad and be-mournful occasion, showing that life indeed must go on despite the tragedies that so often cause us much sorrow and upset our very way of life.

Little did I know at that time, that the essence of this sermon would become so relevant to our situation and would be a useful tool for me in my attempt to encourage the family to keep on living in spite of the tragedy that they had experienced. I had no way of knowing that it would also serve as a stimulant for survival for our grieving mother and family just a few years later.

After our tragedy this determination seemed to prevail throughout our family. Ida Bell went on to receive her Bachelor's degree from Spelman College, and soon thereafter was married. Joe continued his study at Alabama State University and received his Bachelor's of Science degree in Mathematics, with high honors. Of his many job offers, he accepted a position with the fast growing computer industry, I.B.M, and was relocated to Kingston New York. Only Richard and Jimmy were left living at home with mom.

In the meantime, I continued my study at Selma University, and graduated the next year with the Bachelors of Theology degree (Bth). I also continued to teach in the Religious department at the university. At the same time of graduation, I also received the call to pastor the Ebenezer Baptist Church in Auburn, — of which as of the time of this writing- I have pastored for more than thirty-six years, with no retirement intention in mind.

With such painful memory associated with the house on Pleasant Avenue, mother was motivated to move from there a few months after the tragedy. As beneficent of Mr. Paul's Social Security and Retirement funds, she was well able to afford a house or an apartment, despite the fact that because of a, "Suicide Clause", his life insurance didn't pay off. Later our brother Joe and I helped her raise a reasonable down payment on a house on Japonica Street, which became the home house for her and the family until she passed away in October 1991.

Having the children rallying closely around her, Mother soon bounced back to her old self again. In fact, she became even more expressive of her love and affection for the family than ever before. The ever-growing circle of grandchildren, other relatives and their friends added to the original number of children made each holiday a happy and festival occasion. We would all gather at her house for a meal that was literally "fit for a king" all made possible, as each household would contribute some prepared dish for the feast. Mom was always the center of attention and she seemed to be happier than ever having all of us gather at her house. In fact she often remarked that no mother anywhere in this world could possibly be happier than she was. Such was the custom every holiday and sometimes even on weekends when there was nothing special to celebrate.

While each and every one of these gatherings were very significant, the Christmas seasonal celebrations was absolutely the greatest, and were marked by two Yule-tide traditions that were practiced over the years. First: At a family gathering, weeks in advance of Christmas, each person, young and old, would draw from a compilation of names a person's name to whom he or she would be responsible to give a gift for Christmas. These gifts would be placed under a tree at mother's house as they were made or bought, and on Christmas Eve would be given out to the jubilant crowd of anxious children and grownups as well.

Usually I was deputized to play the Santa Claus' role, as someone would always give me a Santa's bonnie and declare that I was the real Santa Claus, which some of the younger children called me long after Christmas was over. With a Ho; Ho; Ho; I would roar out the names one after another until all the gifts were given out. We would then open them with great admiration whether we liked them or not. Like always, Mom was the center of attractions at these events and always ended up with more gifts than anyone else.

Everyone would give her their undivided attention as she opened her gifts trying hard not to make the persons giving the smallest gift feel any less appreciated than those giving the larger ones. With all gifts passed out and opened, we would gather in small groups for playing games for additional gifts, singing a few Christmas carols and sampling some of the seasonal goodies that were always in abundance just about anywhere throughout the house during this season of the year. After returning home for the night, most of us would meet again for the traditional dinner at mother's house on Christmas day.

The next most memorable tradition was held at our house. Since we lived outside the city limits, we would have a large bonfire each year a few days just before Christmas Eve. The entire family and friends would come, some bearing gifts to be passed out to the children. Others bringing their favorite drinks, both alcoholic and non-alcoholic. No one seemed to care, since it was usually held on the coldest night of the week just before Christmas Eve. (The colder it was the better.) And the drinks both tended to make them warmer for the cold night as well as a bit merrier for the season.

Michael and Valerie would help me prepare for the outside event. We would pile logs high in a pile near the brooks edge a distance from the house. I would light the fire far in advance of the arrival of the guest so that it would be a heated inferno by nightfall and the time of their arrival. We would then string Christmas lights from the low hanging limbs of Sweet gum and Oak trees that filled our large lot. Large hand-made Piñatas filled with sorted candies; small toys and other goodies were intermittently hung on other limbs of the nearby trees.

The wood for the fire was piled in front of an over-size storage house that I had built on the lot. This house was complete with a hard wood floor and a metal fireplace in one corner. The fact that I had built it all by myself made it sort of special interest to the rest of the family. More over, with its soft colored lights from red or green bulbs in the center ceiling outlet along with seasonal music blasting from the stereo, it served as the center of activities near the roaring bonfire. We would always build a fire in its fireplace adding to the coziness of the house as the bonfire blazed only a few feet from its opened door. In fact, one night the fire in the metal fireplace became so hot that the house itself caught fire when a board that had been nailed too closely to the briny hot flute became aflame, which was quickly extinguished with a nearby water hose kept close and ready for just such purpose. Everyone joined in playing firemen, even sounding like sirens and fire bells and some simulating newscasters from nearby T.V. stations covering the excitement of the flaming incident. The board was immediately ripped away from the flute and the party continued as if nothing had ever happened.

The children and I also made luminaries of white or brown paper bags, each filled with just enough sand to hold a candle. These also encircled the lot beneath the lights hanging on the tree limbs. Some were placed along both sides of the drive way and walk way leading to the front of the house, and was lit at first night giving an enchanted

173

glow as the December sun set beyond the tall trees to the west, giving an unfelt seasonal chill to the whole Yule-tide scene.

Mamie would be busy inside spending hours on hours in the kitchen preparing little dainties, which she proudly made available to the shivering and excited crowd as they gathered by the car load at different unscheduled times before the fun began. She would make available too some of her prized pickled green tomatoes, or preserved watermelon rinds; along with some cookies that she made with special care, and always a steaming pot of her special made "Russian Tea," which was so well liked that it always ran out long before the party was over. She would become so enthusiastically involved until you couldn't tell that she was so tired and felt so awfully bad just before she commenced to prepare these tasty delights. She sometimes got so involved in the celebration that she even danced or used her musical skills by leading us in the singing of several of the loudly sung Christmas carols which we sang by the fireside inside the family house, and sometimes before the crowd grew too large, we sang in the house while she played on the piano.

One by one carloads of our Yuletide guest arrived. Some following the luminaries went directly into the family house, while others walked past the house and came straight to the blazing fire on the far away back lawn, or filing into the cozy storage house flooded with soft light and Christmas carols blasting from the stereo. They helped themselves to steaming hot popcorn that was still popping on a table in the corner and a steaming cup of Mamie's Russian Tea. In a matter of minutes the whole yard was alive with children wrestling together on piles of pine needles or un-raked sweet gum and oak leaves that afforded a natural carpet under the blinking Christmas lights strung across the wide opened lot. Grownups sitting on makeshift benches and chairs before the open fire, talked and dreamed of bygone days as they toasted marshmallows and roasted wieners skewed on bards of wire made from straighten out clothe hangers amidst thousand of angry sparks that rapidly ascended into the over-head darkness from the blazing logs flaming on the burning pile before them.

In a matter of time everyone, children and grownups, would gather before the fire for a joyful period of carol singing and games playing. Different ones would take terms leading the many songs, but the one in which most became involved in was "Twelve Days of Christmas" It was always very interesting watching the different choral groups sing over and over what their true love gave to them on certain days of Christmas, some forgetting their parts while others sang all parts as though all verses were theirs.

When the celebration was in full force, all the children and grownups would gather under one of the large piñatas and watch blindfolded children attack them one by one, with long poles after they had been spurned around loosing all sense of direction as to just where it was hanging. Often the spectators got smacked many times before the piñata was found. Some times the children would perform on a makeshift stage, reciting Christmas poems and sayings that they had learned at school, singing carols or just horsing around to gain the laughter of the older children and adults.

Before the night was over, someone would change the music on the stereo from carols to music suitable for dancing. Many would rush into the storage house to do their special dance; some steps and music were old and outdated from a time of long long ago, while others were in tune with the children that were by far too energized for

175

grownups such as myself, and people of older generations to appreciate. All the time some were still outside beside the glowing bonfire, roasting wieners and toasting marshmallows, the aroma of which, coupled with that of cooking popcorn gave the night a smell that made one glad to be alive.

Such were the practices of the family from year to year, until mom became too feeble to endure the cold December night air. She spent her last two years celebrating with us by remaining in the house, only venturing onto the lawn for a brief spell before returning to the warmth therein where she would remain until the party was over.

Sometime before midnight every thing ended and everyone left for home anxiously looking forward to the next year and the yard party that had undoubtedly, become quite a tradition for our ever-growing circle of family and friends.

#12. Michael's school picture

177

Valerie, First Grade photo

P146. Valerie's Senior picture.

#13 My graduation picture from Selma University

Chapter 16

A Period of Trials, Challenges and Triumphs

Like a receding storm cloud, time moved on. And all too soon, the children grew up and entered junior high and high school. Mamie continued her teaching career in the Autauga County public school system. I continued my pastorate at the Ebenezer Baptist Church at Auburn as well as teaching in the Religious Department at Selma University.

Of course, since the university was under the sponsorship of the Alabama Baptist State Convention, each affiliated church and pastor of that body should have had equal privileges and rights. But I was soon to learn that this was not necessarily the case in this organization. There seemed to have been a gross misuse of power and discriminating favoritism practiced through out this sacred fellowship, as you may conclude from the reading of this account.

As you may recall, I began teaching in this department in 1969 while still a student at S.U. Upon graduating in 1971, I was added as a full-time member of the faculty, where I remained until I was terminated at the beginning of the fall semester in 1973, for reasons that are yet to be fully explained to me. (This was the first of three times that I would be fired from S.U. during my professional career) Of course, this was very devastating to me as I had set my heart on a teaching career there for a long long time, plus I was convinced that I was a pretty good teacher at that.

At the end of the school year, in May, three months earlier, I had been highly complemented by the university's president and the academic dean for the great work that I was doing as a teacher, and was assured that they expected me to return for the fall semester in September of that year. I spent the greater part of my summer researching; gathering materials and working on lesson plans for the upcoming semester. Only to learn upon my arrival on campus at the beginning of the semester, that my contract had not been renewed, and that I would not be given a teaching assignment at the university.

After a brief period of anger and frustration, I was informed by the dean that I had been singled out and ordered to be fired by the president of the Alabama Baptist State Convention's president, who with a "tribal chief" or a "God Father" mentality, acted out of a personal vendetta in retaliation for a conflict between himself and me, which took place in our local district association in Montgomery, long before he became president of the convention. You see, I had successfully organized and led a correlation of younger pastors in breaking up a monopolizing stronghold of older pastors who had been in office for, what seemed to have been forever. We younger pastors were convinced that they were only using us to "bring in the money". While the president's position as vice moderator was not challenged, he knew that we held the power to move him also. However, we never interfered with his position as vice moderator of our district association which he held until he was elected president of our state convention after the death of his predecessor several years later.

Because of this defying but proper act, many years later, the now, president insisted on firing me, even over the pleading of the president and dean on my behalf, informing him that I was by far, the best instructor in our department. Further more, they told him that they needed at least three additional teachers in order to adequately serve the influx of new students that they were expecting, rather than getting rid of one that they already had. However, despite their pleading protests, he insisted that they would have to get along without me. So, whatever the case, I was fired from the one job that meant so much to me. Of course, I knew that I would be better off financially, because of my release, for my up-keep while teaching there cost me more than I made while teaching from month to month. It was never the less, a rather devastating "slap in the face" when I, without a contract, was compelled to leave and return home to Montgomery.

I utilized the time on hand by extending my, "on the field work" and office hours at the church and in its surrounding areas; also by increasing my preaching activities in revivals and other such church functions. I also utilized my previous missionary skills by organizing and conduction Vacation Bible schools throughout a wide area in and around the state. And since I had also been attending extension classes from Alabama State University at night on the campus of Selma University, I also took advantage of the opportunity to continue my education in pursuit of an academic degree in Sociology, on the campus. I still had quite a few hours of tuitions remaining on my GI bill education grant.

Trials and Challenges at A.S.U.

My study at A.S.U. would also prove to be a most trying experience for me. For, I would be caught in the crossfire between two rivaling department heads at the school. Namely, the professor who directed the extension centers and the one that was over the Department of Veterans Affairs at the school, to whom students at the university had given the nickname "The Hawk". I never knew the nature of the origin of their feudal relationship. I only knew of the sleaziness and bitterness that they had for each other; and that I somehow was caught in the middle of it all. And it was long after I had been having serious and relentless problems concerning my course credits reported to the Alabama State's office of Veterans Affairs down town, before I knew just what was going on.

I had completed four classes the previous quarter in the extension center. I had received official grade reports from the office of the Registrar, certifying that I had earned an "A" in each of the four classes. However, several weeks later, I was shocked when I received a letter from the Office of Veteran's Affair, demanding that I refund the tuitions monies that I had been paid, since it was reported that I had not attended school at all that quarter. I reported this to the director of extension centers, who sent a letter to Veteran's Affairs informing them that I had indeed been enrolled and had satisfactorily completed all course requirements for all four classes attempted. "The Hawk" sent a letter of rebuttal stating that no matter who said what, I was not in school. I then made a visit to the office carrying my grade report, feeling that this would settle the matter. Whereupon, the representative after examining it appeared just as confused as I was. He asked me, "Muse, what in the hell is going on over there?" Of course, I couldn't answer him. He then informed me that while it was evident that I had successfully completed the quarter. He said, unfortunately, he had to recognize the correspondences from our representative over there since he was the official liaison officer between his office and the university. Totally frustrated, I made a visit to the Registrar's office at the university who also informed me that my grade report had been revoked until further notice from the office of Veteran's Affairs of the school.

In total desperation, I made several attempts to meet with the president of the university. Each time, I was informed that he was tired up and couldn't possibly honor my appointment to see him, even though I could clearly see through the open door that he was just sitting at his desk doing nothing and with no one else in the office with him. Angrily, this time, I left his office after telling his secretary to tell him for me, that I would not attempt to see him again, and that my lawyer would be contacting him very shortly.

Once more, I visited the office of the Director of Extensions service. I was then made aware of the ongoing feud and bad blood flowing between him and the "Hawk". He also advised me to get myself the best lawyer possible and that he would split the fee with me no matter the cost. I also had conferences with each of the instructors who taught me that quarter, each were willing to write depositions or appear in court on my behalf, should I need them.

One instructor told me that I had made a mistake by trying to be a gentleman when dealing with office personnel at the school. He said. "Reverend, when I go into any office on campus, I satiate the room with some "damns" before I even tell them what I came in there for," He said, "I throw a few damns over their heads and then across and under the tables and desks, and a few in every nook and corner, by then they tend to respect me more and listen to what ever I have to say. And if that doesn't work" he said, "I start all over again. And pretty soon, they get the message and cooperate with me."

After having built what I felt was an airtight case, on the morning that I was prepared to contract a lawyer. I received an early morning call from the Chairman of Extension centers. He informed me that I had already won my case. I told him that I couldn't have possibly won when I hadn't as yet gone to court, and that I was in the process of contacting a lawyer to handle my case even as we spoke. He pleaded for me to trust him just this once more and go by the Registrar's office for the final conclusion of my case. When I refused to comply, he informed me that the president had called a special faculty and staff meeting in which he ordered the "Hawk" "to do whatever he must do to satisfy Reverend Muse, for he is about to take this school to court, and he is sure to win. But the university will not suffer loss, you will." The chairman then reminded me of his willingness to help me secure a lawyer and that he would still help me, but that he saw no reason for an "overkill" plus said he, "Every staff and faculty member on this campus know Reverend W. L. Muse now." He said "Just go by that office this once more for me." After consenting to do so I proceeded to physically and mentally prepare myself for this drudgerous task.

In route to campus, I spent considerable time reflecting of some hot "damns" that I could use when I arrived at the Registrar's office, as my professor had suggested. However, I just couldn't quite bring myself around to it. You may remember that back home on the plantation, Mr. "X" often used curse words that almost made "fig trees wither." So you see, I knew some curse words from having listened to his outrageous vulgarity for so many years. But I just somehow couldn't bring myself around to using them on an old man who was clearly under the spell of the "Hawk" and was at no time acting on his own.

Once in the office, I couldn't help but notice the nervousness of the registrar. With trembling hand, he reached for a record book he had placed on a table in the center of the room as he anticipated my arrival. We never shook hands nor looked each other directly in the eye. He commenced to explain that he didn't know that I was a minister and attempted to explain that the university had experienced some serious problems in the past and therefore was compelled to use extra precautions in order to avoid a repeated occurrence. He used just about every excuse possible without stating the real reason for his action toward me, which was, that he was under the spell of the "Hawk."

I therefore, anxiously seized the first opportunity to sling some "damns" in his direction. I barked "It shouldn't have mattered a tinker's damn to you whether I was a minister or not. The only thing that should have mattered to you was the fact that I was a student, and as such I should have been treated fairly and with due respect. Furthermore, so far as my concern about the university's problem with the V.A., I simply couldn't care less if they had closed this diver's den down. All I want of you is a certified copy of verification of my grades so I can get the hell out of this God forsaken place." Whereupon, he carefully prepared fresh copies of my records affixed with the official seal of his office. I swiftly jerked it from his hand, even as he pointed out the corrections that he had made in the records book. He also assured me that he would make it right with the

Veteran's Affair office down town. I immediately left his office slamming the door behind me as I did so.

I saw the "Hawk" several years later, after his retirement from the university as he sat and ate alone in a local restaurant. He clothes was shabbily hanging from his slumping shoulders. Even though a few people waved to him and verbally greeted him from a distance, no one even attempted to join him as he sat alone, starring as if he wished so badly for someone to befriend him. A few years later his obituary was carried in the local newspaper, and just like that, the "Hawk" was gone and was seen no more. Several years later both the College President and the Chairman of Extensions services were also laid to rest. With this, I sadly bring this chapter of the saga relating to him to an infamous end.

In spite of all, I continued my studies at Alabama State University, and graduated in the spring of 1977 with a degree in Sociology and a minor in Psychology. After graduation I was immediately asked to return to Selma University to resume my teaching career in the department of Religion. I remained there until 1985 when I was let go in such a way as to constitute the second time that I was fired from that institution.

Meanwhile, the children continued to grow up and completed high school, with Michael finishing in 1980, five years before Valerie. He entered Morehouse College in Atlanta. He and Pat got married the third year of his college experience. At the time of his graduation, (1984) Valerie was also graduating from high school, and the next year she enrolled at Alabama A. & M. University in Huntsville. With that, both children for the most part, had deserted the "nest" leaving Mamie and me home alone for the first time since we were married. Of course, I was home mostly on weekends and holidays, as I had secured an apartment in Selma, where I lived during the week while teaching there.

Fired From Selma University the Second Time

My second release from S.U. in 1985 was almost a repeat performance of the first. I had finished the 1984 fall semester in December with the expectation of returning in January, a few weeks later, to resume the spring semester. Early in January before the semester began, I returned to the school to prepare for my classes.

Upon my arrival on campus, I was surprised to learn that the president was already in his office. He was a different president and much younger than the one was there when I was fired before. He had a laugh that reminded me of a cackling rooster. This reminded me of something Mama Lillie often told us when we were young, "a person that laugh a lot also tells a whole lot of lies." And he was just about as reliable as a broken walking stick in the hand of a five hundred pound cripple. But he did have a bit of charisma that gave some promise that he could lead the school out of the slump that it had been in for more than a decade.

As I mounted the stairs to climb up to my office located on the third floor, the president called me to his office, which was located on the first floor of the building. Once there, he said to me "Muse, you know you have to go back to school don't you?" I asked him "when?" "Now, this semester" He said. I asked him "Why now, and not later, since my daughter just enrolled in college and the two of us can't afford to go to college at the same time? "Will the school assist me with tuitions and other expenses, since I will be bettering myself to continue teaching here?" I asked. He said "No, for you will be going back to school to help yourself and not to help the university."

After informing him that I will be going to school on my own since I have always intended to return in pursuit of the higher degree. But never quite found the time to do so, since I was always teaching at the college even before I graduated with the degree in Theology. I continued, "But once I get this degree, you can be assured that I will never even look in the direction of Selma University again." Having said this, I hastened from his office and with a heavy heart, climbed the stairs to the third floor to clear my office of my personal effects.

I had hauled about three armfuls of cardboard boxes down and placed them in the car. I was returning the fourth climb the president once again called me by his office. This time he tried to compromise with me by prefacing his statement something like this: "Doc, I don't want you to leave here angry with me for you are my best teacher that I have in that department," He said "I will try to help you with your expenses in seminary, if you will recruit students for us, while you are in school. Let's say, in your spare time." Why anybody pastoring a church and attending seminary some one hundred and fifty miles away, knows that there will be no possible spare time for anything else, much less to recruit students. Of course, this was only his way of trying to scapegoat his way over a tough situation. Of course, I knew that he never intended to fulfill his promise to me in the first place.

After loading my belongings, I sadly left the campus, determining never to even look that way again. Once home, I called the registrar's office at the Interdenominational Theological Center in Atlanta in search for the requirements for immediate enrollment in the Master's program there. I was shocked to learn that presemester enrollment had taken place in November and had already been closed for that semester. I was informed however; that since I was an instructor at Selma University that special provision would be made for me to enroll. However to do so, I would have to be on campus on the following Monday morning at 8:00 A.M. to take a battery of entrance exams. To fail to meet these conditions would result in my having to wait until the next semester to enter.

I therefore rushed to make preparation to leave on Sunday, after a fellow pastor who was also interested in enrolling got out of evening service. He and I had planned to travel together to Atlanta, leaving at 8:00 P.M. As luck would have it, at 6:00, Mamie got a call from Prattville that her mother had taken seriously ill. She immediately left home rushing to be at her side. Once in Prattville, she called wailing and weeping informing me that her mother was at the point of death. She died just as she arrived or in route to the hospital before 7:00 P.M. I rushed over Prattville to be at her side and to offer such comfort as I could to her during this awful time. I remained with her most of the night assisting her as she continuously made telephone calls informing family members and friends of her passing, many of whom lived in distant cities far beyond Prattville.

Realizing that I had to be in Atlanta by eight o'clock in the morning, which was only a few hours away, Mamie insisted that I go home and at least get some rest before taking the drive. I went home and went to bed, but of course, due to all the grief and excitement, I got very little sleep before it was time for me to get up and hit the road for Atlanta. As you can imagine, I certainly was not in any condition to take those all-important tests after I arrived in

Atlanta during the early morning rush hours traffic, especially since they would last all that day.

Trials and Challenges at the I.T.C.

I did rather well on all the tests except for English, which I attributed to my having had no sleep since Saturday night. By the time I took that test late in the afternoon on Monday, I couldn't distinguish a verb from a noun or an adverb from a preposition. In fact, I did so poorly on it until the rather inconsiderate instructor demanded that I take a full semester of remedial English. Although I knew that I needed to brush up on my English a bit, I strongly protested having to spend a whole semester in that effort. But I ended up doing just that. And by doing so I was greatly benefited even more than I, out of my personal pride, would like to admit, for my involvement in the weekly class sessions along with the frequent essays that I was required to write did more than just meet the demands of the instructor, they also created a sort of hunger in me to write even more. Before then I found this to be a most drudgerous and laborious task at best.

By the end of the day I was informed that I had successfully completed all exams, and I, along with the other seminarians was extended a heartily welcome by the president, faculty and staff of the institution. The next day I commenced to attend classes as a full time student, taking remedial English three hours on Fridays that semester.

With that, apart from the well-attended funeral, which took place that weekend, I had embarked upon a routine of life that would last for the next three years. Three years of juggling meager resources between paying my daughter's tuitions and mine. Three years of burning the highway in the very early morning hours each Monday in the attempt to beat the early morning traffic rush in order to meet an eight o'clock class in Atlanta, a hundred and fifty miles from Montgomery. Three years of repeating boring and uninteresting classes that I had already taken (or taught) on a lower level while studying for the Bachelor's of Theology degree at Selma University and beyond.

One dear professor implied that my being required to take these courses was tantamount to me being punished for not having gone to that institution (I.T.C.) in the first place. He also asked the class the question, "Class, What can I teach Reverend Muse, who has been preaching, pastoring and teaching just about as long as I have and is probably just as well read?" Of course, I was exempted from much of his classroom requirements since he felt that I didn't need to be held to the same requirements as other students. I only had to participate in special class projects and take the required exams as dictated by the institution. Most other professors however, were not quite so considerate toward me. Never the less, I had my heart and mind set upon getting this degree, therefore I would allow nothing short of death, a serious accident or some debilitating illness to prevent my doing so. Therefore, I toughened up and determined to keep fighting to the end come rain of come shine.

Each day brought new and greater challenges for me. First there was the challenge of meeting new and exciting students, both male and females, from across the nation as well as from the continent of Africa. Then there was the excitement of studying with students across five or more denominational lines, where we were both able to compare and study the various doctrines of each other's church, just as we studied the common doctrines that we shared, which held us together as unified Christian fellowships.

But the greatest of all challenges was that of trying to meet financial deadlines in order to remain in school. For this I often prayed for divine intervention and help in meeting this obligation. One such instance was during my first semester, after I had been in school for only a month. The business office informed me that unless I paid the total tuitions of $2500.00 by a certain time that I would be dismissed from school. I had no earthly means to raise this money by the deadline date. It was then that I seriously went into prayer, telling the Lord that while I didn't know just how he would do it. But that I knew that somehow, he would.

Having done this, I just stood by and waited on Him. Then, suddenly, the worst February ice and snow storm hit our region, dropping temperature to an all time low and causing much wintry havoc by bursting pipes in unheated buildings and homes from Maine to California, sending both people and animals scurrying for cover into or under any place that could shield them from the wintry blast. The storm came suddenly and left just as suddenly, leaving in its wake immeasurable damage and destruction. Nevertheless, it also provided an answer to the prayer that I had prayed, seemly a thousand times or more.

Our house was not spared from this terrible catastrophe, for when Mamie got home from school that evening she was greeted by ankle-deep water standing on the floors throughout the house. A water pipe had ruptured in the outer wall of a bedroom and the water had run throughout the house after thawing sometime during the day. The neighbors were helping her mop up the mess when she called to inform me about it. I found myself wondering just how the Lord could allow this to happen to me at such a time as this, even at a time when nothing seemed to have been going right in my life. Mamie seemed contented enough as she reminded me of the fact that she had always wanted to change from the hardwood parquets tile to a full house of carpet. So she contacted the insurance carrier who readily agreed to the change, citing that the carpet was less costly than the tile anyway. After the adjustment, you will never guest, we had $2500.00 left over, the exact amount for which I had prayed and trusted the Lord for. Once again, He had turned a terrible disaster into an awesome blessing in disguise for me, thus enabling me to remain in school yet a little while longer.

Only a few months later, I found myself in the very same predicament. Once again I was threatened with dismissal from school for lack of boarding and tuition payments. And like the first time, I once again found myself on my knees praying for a solution to, what to me was an impossible situation. Once again I found myself praying and trusting the Lord for the $ 1200.00 that I needed to remain in school. January 15th, on Dr. Martin Luther King's birthday, as I was driving on one of the very busy arteries near the airport in Atlanta, when out of nowhere, an inebriated woman struck me on the passenger side as I was making a left turn. The damage to my car was very extensive and it was assessed just short of being a total loss. Although neither the woman nor I sustained any injury in the collision, this was an insurmountable blow for me, for I had lost my only means of transportation, in addition I was in dire need of overdue boarding and tuition funds. Therefore I needed to buy a car plus raise the other needed funds. My excellent credit allowed me to purchase a used Toyota from a local car dealer, but raising the funds was yet to be reckoned with if I was to continue in school.

It turned out that the woman had valid insurance, which paid for the repairs on my car. After negotiating with auto repairmen from Atlanta to South Carolina, I finally settled on one who could assure me that he could fix the car for such an amount that would leave me the $1200. 00 that I needed to pay my bill. Once again, although as painful as it was, my prayer had been answered, and I was able to remain in school. However, by this time I began to question the Lord as to why he, while answering all my prayers, always answered them in such painful ways? I however took personal comfort in knowing that once again, the Lord had kept his promise by keeping me in all my ways if my mind always stayed on Him.

On the very night of the accident, Mamie called, even before I returned to campus and left word for me to call her at home. When I did so her she informed me that Valerie was attempting to register for the new semester at A. &. M. And that she had gone as far as they would allow her to go in this process until her tuitions were prepaid in full. She also informed me that we had only $3000.00 dollars in our savings account, which was the exact amount that was needed. I agreed that we would draw it out and wire it to her immediately. Having done this we were completely broke, but happy that once again the Lord had made it possible for her to remain in school for yet a few months more.

In the meanwhile, our son Michael had been granted a scholarship to New Orleans Theological Seminary. He and his family had moved there, while he studied at the seminary, he was also assigned to pastor a small mission church just outside the city. Strangely, for several months he had been suffering severe headaches, which his doctors concluded was only due to stress of too much activity inside and outside the classroom. One evening he decided to go to the Mardi Gras, and while there; a runaway car that was thought to have been driven by a drunken man struck him. He was rushed by ambulance to the hospital. Once there, the doctors discovered that while he received no injury from the accident, that he did however, have a very serious pituitary gland problem, which without immediate surgery could prove fatal for him in a matter of four to five months. The doctors then concluded that this was the cause of his previous headaches. He immediately under went surgery. After recovering, he continued his studies at the seminary, while he continued pastoring the mission church until he graduated. Upon graduation he opted to transfer to Ames, Iowa, where he planted the first Black church on the Iowa State University's campus. Once again the mighty hand of the Lord was seen intervening in our family's affairs.

Amidst all of this, I continued my struggle to stay in school. It seemed that every time I paid one bill there were always larger and more urgent ones that demanded monies that I couldn't afford or didn't have.

I did however; get a flash of encouragement upon the arrival of a new dean at the school. He was an ordained clergyman of the Baptist denomination and had full knowledge of the quality of students and leaders that Selma University had produced for more than a century, even though it had never been accredited as a college. He knew that pastors who graduated from that institution pastored some of the larger Baptist churches across the nation. He also knew that its students have always been able to defend themselves in the academic and religious arena wherever they went.

Upon reviewing my records along with another student who had also graduated from Selma and Alabama State University like myself, he ordered the Registrar to reduce the number of hours that we were required to take, which should have reduced my tenure there by one full year. However by the time this action was taken, I was well into the third year. The most that my requirement was reduced was only by one semester. The dean also ordered the Registrar to place this ruling in the records so that any student with similar qualifications would automatically be given the same consideration.

This having been done, graduation day was moved up for me and was approaching far too soon for me to raise the necessary fund to clear up my indebtedness by that long-awaited day. I know that by now I should have had full confidence that the Lord would come through for me just as he had done so many times since I began this pursuit. Nevertheless, I still mustered up some anxiety not knowing just how He would do it.

This time he used my dear mother as the catalyst. As I visited her on one of my "down" days, she noticed that I seemed very tired or quite ill. When I assured her that while I was somewhat tired, I was not sick. I continued by telling her of my rapidly approaching graduation day and that I was somewhat perplexed as to how I could raise the needed funds by that time. She then insisted that I give her my address, preferably a nearby post office address. She comforted me by assuring me that everything would be all right.

The next week I received from her a letter containing a small money order in the amount of $35.00, which she had sent from her very meager resources, which I knew that she could barely afford, since she had recently under gone surgery for some form of cancer and was presently undergoing chemotherapy on a regular basis. To me her gift was so sacred that I had an awful time seeing it through my eyes, which were flooded with tears, much less spending it. I immediately associated this with the "Widow's Mite" as experienced by Jesus in the gospels, for to me she had given all that she could to help me during this awful time in my life.

When I returned home that weekend, she called me to tell me that she had something for me and that I should come by as soon as possible. When I got there she presented an envelope to me explaining that Minnie, one of my sisters, had left it with her for me, and that she didn't know just why she had left a card for me since it was Mother's Day and she hadn't given her a card. When I opened the card, I almost wept aloud, for she had included a crisp $50.00 bill along with a note that said, "This is for your dinner only, enjoy it and don't worry about any bills that you may have, for we, your sisters and brothers whom you brought from the country will raise whatever money you may need for graduation, for we can never thank you enough for all that you have done for us." She continued, "Just who do you think paid my tuitions when I was in Trade school? You did." she answered. "When we needed money for food or doctor's bill, or medicine, we had to look to you and you always came through for us." She added. So you should have known better than to be suffering for money and not tell us about it."

She concluded, "Mother also informed me that you have some kind of paper to write before you graduate. I have a friend who is experienced in writing term papers and other such papers as you may need, (of course, I was required to write a "critical essay" by my "most critical" advisor) My friend has consented to help you with it," she said. "All she wants from you is the theme on which you must write and the date that it is due. And all we want is for you to complete your degree and graduate, for after all, you will be the first of the family to receive the Master's degree." Needless to say, their compassionate concern had such an impact on me that it was many months before I could talk about it, even from the pulpit, without openly shedding blinding tears.

The next few days leading up to graduation moved rather rapidly. And even though I had long anxiously anticipated it, every day brought on new and exciting challenges. First, there was the matter of completing class assignments as required for each course. Then, there were final exams, which, of all things, really confirmed that the time of my departure was near. And finally, there were friends and acquaintances along with concerned professors that had supported me all the while that I was there through their lasting friendship and professional counseling that I had to adjust to leaving behind. But be it as it may, the time for graduation was at hand and boy was I ready for it?

The final week was upon us and I had finished all of my course work and final exams, except one, which was to be on Wednesday of that week. My family had given to me the money that I needed for clearing my financial obligations, which they together had raised by having fish fries and by casting in their personal financial contributions toward this effort. My dear wife, Mamie, and the children also joined them in the pursuit of accomplishing this goal.

My sister's friend had also delivered the critical essay that I had to turn in before I would be cleared for graduation.

Of course the professor upon receiving it, gave me the toughest of time, penalizing me for just about everything, from using too many comas to not using enough colons, semicolons or quotation marks, before finally approving the paper; And that was only after I threaten him telling him that "I intended to graduate, and on time, or else." He then assured me that he would get me out of there on time.

In the mean time, a long-time friend of mine, who pastor a rather large church in Miami, called and asked if I would come down to be his guest minister for a special service on the next Sunday. He asked that I would come soon after my last exam on Wednesday, in order that I may get some badly needed rest before Sunday. Of course I obliged him, and as soon as the exam was over, I left Atlanta for Miami. I had made plans with the family to drive back to Montgomery to pick them up for the next Saturday's graduation. My friend was rather generous toward me, insisting that I park my car once there and he driving me in his limo from the time I arrived on Wednesday, until just before I left on Monday, of the next week. He also gave me a sizable financial contribution after the Sunday's service, and even offering me more if I thought that this was not enough. Of course, I somewhat felt that he had already over paid me when I considered all the things that he had done for me since my arrival, which included taking care of my hotel fare, plus five days of wining and dining at some of Miami's best restaurants.

Leaving Miami early Monday morning, I returned to Montgomery to pull together such loose ends as I needed to for Saturday's graduation. I then left for Atlanta on Thursday, as I had some last minute business to take care of on Friday, the day before that glorious event. Members of the family and some friends agreed to join me at a local hotel in Atlanta on Friday, where we would all have dinner together and spend the night.

My excited guest began arriving about midday on Friday as planned, and throughout the rest of the day they kept trickling in until by mid evening there was a festival atmosphere existing throughout the corridors of the entire hotel, giving me a sense of special importance that I, here-to-fore, had never known, (even though there were families and guests of other graduating students were also there.) While I was very excited by the presence of everyone that came, I was most thankful that mother had felt well enough to join us, for her presence gave special meaning to the whole affair of my celebration. After a hardy and most enjoyable dinner in the hotel's dining room, we spent a few hours socializing before we all departed for our rooms to get some badly needed rest and sleep before the next morning's climatic excitement.

Saturday morning, the big day finally arrived. Like bees in a hive, we all were busy getting dressed for the graduation exercise. After checking out of the hotel we made our way through the busy early morning traffic to the Morehouse college campus where the graduation would take place in the Martin Luther King Memorial Chapel, a very elaborate and imposing building that was used by all the colleges of the Atlanta University center when they had activities that were too large for them to accommodated in their own chapters. Therefore the I.T.C. with the largest class to graduate in many years was using these facilities today in anticipation of a near record attendance.

When we emerged from the dressing room amidst the large crowd of congregants, I couldn't help but notice that my already sizable delegate of family and friends had grown even larger with the arrival of a sizable number of members from the church that I pastored in Auburn. They all stood near the entry way in a huddle to make sure that I would see them before the ceremonies began. And while the bright May sunlight flooded them, to me there seemed to have been a special ray of light beaming upon them high lighting them from the rest of the anxious crowd that was there. Needless to say, I felt, as I was ten feet taller by all this attention, of which I was at least, their main attraction.

The ceremony began and after several lively numbers by bands and choral groups and a brief but appropriate address, my long awaited time had come. When my name was called I hastened across the stage amidst a loud out burst of applauses and screams, to receive the degree. When I looked around my entire entourage of family, friends and church members were all standing and applauding me for my great and long-sought-after accomplishment. I marched across that stage having all bills paid and a $ 500.00 check in my pocked that I didn't owe anybody, all made possible by the generosity of my family and a few faithful friends. With that, just as suddenly as it all started in January 1985 at Selma, it was all over in May of 1987, thus we all left Atlanta and headed for "Sweet home Alabama."

After a brief period of catching-up on my pastoral work at the church, which had not developed an appreciation for full-time shepherding. Their demand for the pastor to be in the office every day was a requirement. Therefore after a little rest and recuperation time, it soon became business as usual for me. However, after having to comply with such an arduous schedule for so long, I found it very difficult to adjust to just sitting around, holding my hands and doing nothing. It didn't take very long for me to catch up on the things that I had longed to do during the two and a half years that I was in school, since I did have some time to do some of them on weekends and other such off days that I had during that time.

#12a. Michael, Pat and Tanerica at
Michael's graduation from college.

#12b. Newspaper article, Michael becomes pastor for Dexter Ave. Baptist Church.

New Dexter Avenue pastor challenged, not intimidated

By Laurie A. Lattimore
The Alabama Baptist

HE HAS A DREAM — Following Martin Luther King's legacy as pastor of Dexter Avenue King Memorial Baptist Church, Montgomery, is exciting for Michael Thurmon.

#12c. Newspaper article, Michael becomes pastor for Dexter Ave. Baptist Church.

913a. My graduation picture from I.T.C. Morehouse Atlanta, Georgia

Graduation I T C Atlanta
1987

Rev. Willie L. Muse

Chapter 17

My Final Return to Selma University

It was one of those idle days as I was returning to Montgomery from a trip to Birmingham, that I decided to detour from the main route and drop by Selma for a visit to the school. After all just before I graduated I had heard of the firing of the president who had in fact, dismissed me prior to my entering seminary. And just as a former neighbor of his had predicted two and a half years earlier, when I informed her that he had dismissed me. She said to me, "Son, that boy doesn't know what he is doing messing with you, for I have seen the Lord do too many wonderful and strange things in your life for him to let him get away with that; Just observing your life have made a much stronger believer of me. You go on to school, and I promise you that when you graduate, he will have been long since fired from that school and they will be begging you to come back there to teach."

Arriving at the school, I was warmly greeted by the former Academic dean, now serving as interim president. (He would later become president.) He congratulated me for my recent graduation. And true to the prophecy, his very next words were: "Reverend Muse, you know that you have got to come back to Selma University to teach, don't you? Of course, I informed him of the vow that I made when I was forced to leave there, which was that "I will never even look that way again, let alone come back there to work." He then insisted, that I had no choice, for no matter who leaves or stays, that I had no other choice but to come back, for he nor the school had nothing to do with my dismissal when I was forced to leave. He concluded, "I too have been mistreated from time to time since I have been here, but as you can see, I remained and now you see where I am. Therefore, you have no choice but to come back here to teach." Plus, he said, "The students and I have been anticipating your return since hearing that you were about to finish your schooling. Furthermore, he said, ever since you left we have been awaiting your return."

Being moved by such strong persuasion, I told him to come up with a figure for compensation and give me a little time to think about it, and I would get back to him with my decision within a few days. But as if he already knew what my decision would be, he said, "I will see you on Monday of next week, you will then be informed as to just what classes you will be teaching."

Just as he had said, I returned on Monday, and was just as excited as I had been when I first arrived there the two previous times that I had been hired to teach there. And just like that, I entered there on my third employment, as Instructor at my beloved alma mata, to do that of which I was always assured was my second calling as a Christian minister. My first calling was that of pastoring a church and shepherding the people of God in the spirit of Jesus Christ, just as those faithful pastors had done in shepherding and molding my life. These faithful pastors shepherded me even while I was on the plantation, and have somehow done so, long before and since I became a Christian.

It didn't take very long for me to reestablish a bonding with the students who had previously studied under me. And even some of those that had come while I was away also voiced their anticipation of entering into at least, one of my classes while they were enrolled there. However, such was not the case between my departmental head and me. For some reason, he seemed to have been terribly intimidated by me or resentful of my return. He seemed most resentful particularly when he heard students discussing with much excitement, certain subjects that we had discussed in the various classes when ever they assembled for lunch or some other times as they clustered together somewhere on campus after classes were over. Time and time again, he would show his resentment toward me by taking several of the classes that I was teaching and teaching them himself, without even discussing it with me. He would make me aware of the changes by hand writing it on a sheet of paper and sliding it under my office door while I was away. To make matters worse, he often even used my syllabi and my selected textbooks while he taught the commandeered classes.

Next he took my office, telephone and a desk, which I had retrieved from the trash pile and spent my personal funds refurbishing since there were not enough desks to accommodate all the offices assigned to the instructors. And no resources were available to pay the teachers but a meager salary, much less for purchasing such furniture as was needed. So he felt compelled to just take mine for his own usage. He simply sneered at me saying, "I need that office; I need that desk and telephone." Of course, I felt that all this was uncalled for and a bit evil, since all that I wanted to do was to help the students become more capable to do the work that the Lord had laid upon their hearts to do. I never sought his nor any other position during the entire time that I taught there.

Upon reporting his action to the president, who apologetically stated that he would assign me another office and buy me a desk for the sake of peace. I then assured him that I was more concern about the principle of the matter than about his spending money that he needed for more urgent causes than buying a desk for me. I did however; accept a vacant office in the same building, which was isolated and inconveniently situated on the third floor behind the chapel area in the same building one floor above the office that I previously occupied. And like before, I found and refurbished an old discarded desk for usage in it. A few weeks later several truckloads of surplus furniture arrived on campus and I was the first to be offered a desk by the president, which I refused to accept, making myself content with the one that I had refurbished instead. As far as I know, he never confronted my department head to discuss the principle that was seriously violated in this matter.

This "off the beaten path" office, however, provided me the extra solitude that I needed for study and meditation, as well as provide a place of privacy for me to meet with students who needed my counseling, for situated as it was, seldom did anyone just happened by or just drop in without an appointment. In order to get there one had to climb the three flights of stairs, as the building was not equipped with an elevator.

It was during just such a moment of quiet meditation as I sat in my office, that I heard someone struggling to reach the top of the stairs. I could hear them walk a while and pause briefly for rest. I could even hear them struggling to breathe as I waited and wondered for their arrival. Finally in walked an old revered professor, who had taught in the Religious Department for many years, in fact he taught me as I studied as a student there many years earlier. It was none other than the aged Dr. Fred Chestnut, the only white teacher in that department; in fact he was the only white employed at the school. He was noted for his loving and compassionate spirit and his uncompromising faithfulness in teaching whatever class assigned him to teach.

This was his second visit with me since I moved into this office. His first was several months earlier, when he came up to say to me, " Brother Muse, I see that they are giving you the classes that no one else wants to teach. This is exactly what I have had to do just about all the while that I have been here. However, I have developed syllabi for most of those classes that you are assigned to teach; therefore, I will help you prepare for them." On this visit, after pausing briefly to catch his breath, he said to me, "Brother Muse, The president has indicated that he will expect all members of the faculty and staff to march in the upcoming graduation exercises. I don't know whether I will be able to do so at this time, in fact I don't feel that I will be able to ever march again." He continued, "But whether I am able to do so or not, I want you to have my Academic regalia. If I am able to march I will have it ready for you immediately afterward. If I am not able to do so, I will arrange with my wife for you to pick it up at our home, for I really want you to have it."

Of course, I gratefully thanked him saying, "Dr. Chestnut, I am humbly grateful to you for your unmatchable generosity, as I remember another greater Old Testament prophet who left his mantle to a lesser prophet, and to think that you have thought of me in this regard is more than I can understand. Neither have I the capacity to quite appreciate or express its intricate worth to me." With that he arose and slowly crept out the door to make his less stressful descent down the stairs and out of the building.

A few days later as I was taking my morning bath before leaving my apartment for work, I heard the telephone ring. Already in the tub, I couldn't get to it in time before the answering machine picked up the call. As I listened, my interest was heightened as I detected that it was Dr. Chestnut. He was busily talking, taking frequent intervals to catch his breath. I dared not interrupt the recording, as I didn't want to further tire him. Again he repeated that he wanted me to have his academic regalia, since he would not be able to participate in the graduation exercise, and that I could pick them up from his wife at his home whenever it was convenient for me to do so. Finally, he informed me that he was leaving for the hospital later that morning and desired my prayer for him. Two days later I went to the hospital to see him, as I would be out of the city for the next few days.

Upon arriving at the hospital I was greeted in the hall by his dear wife along with some friends of her's. She informed me that he was very sick and that he was not receiving visitors at that time. However, after I introduced myself, she immediately told me, "Brother Muse, Fred has been expecting you ever since he came to the hospital, and by all means, you must go in to see him. When I entered the room I discovered that he was indeed very sick. But hearing my voice, he livened up a bit and commenced to talk to me. According, to his wife, he talked more than he had done during the entire time he had been in the hospital. Once again he reminded me of his desire for me to have his regalia and that I could arrange to pick it up at a time that was convenience for his wife and me. He then said, "Brother Muse, over the years, there have been three important institutions in my life: My Family; My Church; and Selma University, and I can assure you that I have been faithful to all three of them to the very end." After a brief prayer with him, I quietly left the room knowing that his departure was at hand and even nearer than I had thought before my mid day visit. As I left the hospital grounds, I was quite convinced that this would be the last time that I would see this godly man alive until we meet again in that far off place called heaven.

Early the next morning I left Selma to attend a four-day meeting in Dothan, a hundred and fifty miles away. I could not help but think about my dear friend and kept wondering just how he was getting along. On the fourth day persons arriving from Selma informed me that he had died the day that I left and that his funeral was being held even as they spoke. The shock of the news his passing was made no less by my weeklong expectation, and my being so far away left me to offer to the family my heartfelt condolence, later that evening via telephone, once they were home from the funeral.

Upon returning to Selma I received a call from Mrs. Chestnut informing me as to where she had left the package containing the regalia. When I picked it up I somehow had the distinct feeling that it was too sacred for me to open, much less for my personal usage. I therefore reverently stored it in a special place in the office until such time as I might decide just how best to make use of such precious and sacred items. When I finally was inspired to open it, to my surprise, everything was brand new, the robe, the cap and the stole, and were even still wrapped in the original wrapper as when they were purchased. All were meticulously wrapped and packaged as if he had planned to present them as some kind of offering to a deity or a special son whom he honored and admired so much.

Several months later as I served as interim president of the school, I found them to be a very fitting memorial for him as the entire regalia was enshrined in a glass and wood case. It was specially designed with a polished mahogany cross in the center, upon which these items were draped for permanent display, and set beneath a large imposing photo of his in a small block building across from the campus.

This building had been built for a chapel for him by the white Baptist association and later, after his death, given to Selma University in his memory. This was done with an appropriate ceremony at the receiving and dedication of this building, which were attended by representatives of both black and white Baptists from throughout the Selma, Dallas county area, including members and friends of the Chestnut family. With that our dear friend and Christian mentor was permanently etched, not only in our hearts, but also forever into the minds and memory of all who will gaze upon the likeness of this kind and dedicated servant of our Lord.

In the mean while, graduation services took place at the university, and I surprisingly, along with several other honorees, received honorary degrees for outstanding work that we had done throughout the years. This action completely caught me by surprise. I had wondered just why the president seemed to have been deliberately avoiding me all the while just before the graduation was to take place. He hardly had anything at all to say to me, and even when he did he was short and casual, and very unlike the warm and caring person that I had known him to be.

However he had been in communication with my wife and family who surprisingly showed up on the campus just minutes before the services began. It was only then that the president informed me that I along with another member of our teaching faculty would be awarded honorary degrees. Mamie and Valerie had made the trip, and had brought with them an engraved nameplate for my desk that read "Dr. W. L. Muse." After the services, Valerie jokingly quipped, "Daddy, now you can rightly be called 'doctor,' for before now, you couldn't even have been called a 'foot' doctor." She was referring to the time when she was a little girl and wanted to insist that I was a doctor and when I informed that I was not, she wanted to know if I was not even a 'foot' doctor, when I said no to that, she said to me, "Daddy you know something?" I said, "What?" She said, "You ain't nothing'. Well, this time however, you are most worthy to receive such unique honor from the institution to which you have given so much and from which you have received so little." She said.

#944b. Valaria's college graduation picture.

Chapter 18

Trying Times,
A Wedding and a Funeral

The next three years were most trying for the family and me, since both mother and Mamie; my wife would experience debilitating sickness which would become progressively worse throughout that year, and especially during the last six weeks of mother's life. Mother's cancer would flare up again and again, each time getting worse than the time before, which caused her to become constantly hospitalized until it finally, resulted in her death in October of that year.

In the meantime, our daughter Valerie, after graduating from Alabama A&M University, was employed at Red Stone Arsenal. There she met her future husband, Christopher Sutton. After a brief courtship, Chris came home with her one weekend. And after dinner Valerie said to me, "Daddy, Chris has something that he wants to ask you when you have the time." Later that evening I made myself available to talk with him. He said to me, Reverend Muse, I love your daughter Valerie, and I would like to ask you for her hand in marriage." He later said that I responded to him by saying, "I am not interested in giving you only her hand. If you are going to have any part of her, you must have all of her." (Of course, I don't remember saying it quite that way.) However, I do know that he then replied, "I would like your blessing in giving me all of her to marry."

The next day was Saturday, and he and I went fishing on a small boat that I owned. He was very active and busy while we fished on the Alabama River, until I told him, "Chris, sit your butt down for should you fall out of this boat and drown, I wouldn't want your mother and father to think that after you asked to marry my daughter, that I brought you out here and drowned you." Of course, after a brief laugh, we enjoyed a very pleasant day of fishing, but returning home very late that day having caught nothing.

The wedding was set to take place on August 17th, a year later (1991) at the Ebenezer Baptist Church in Auburn, the church wherein she had grown up since she was five years old. This was the same church, which she gives herself credit for my having been called to pastor when she was only five years old, by telling me that if I wanted the church, "Don't preach too loud and don't preach too long." She was also baptized there had won many friends, among both young and older members of the church, as well as non members who lived in the surrounding communities, during her growing up years.

The day of the wedding finally came. It seemed that nearly every one from Auburn, Opelika, Montgomery and many other areas were present, especially members from the various surrounding churches as well as those from the Ebenezer church family. There were present, to name a few, the entire Sutton family, along with many members of Chris' church, his bishop and a large delegation from the denomination of which his church was affiliated. He was well known, very active and greatly respected in this church throughout his growing up years. One of his father's brothers, who is a minister, would accompany Michael in performing the ceremony, while I being the father, would escort the bride down the aisle to the altar. Many of Valerie's peers from college, along with her friends from Montgomery and elsewhere were also there. Several of them served as bride's maids or played some other significant role in the wedding party.

In the crowd sat many older members from our church who had attributed to the spoiling of her in one way or the other over the years. Some men also contributed to spoiling her by slipping her and Michael a quarter, sometimes a dollar or a bar of candy in gestures to show love and kindness to them through out their childhood and youthful years. The women had often cooked special foods for her in the attempt to "put some meat on her little bony legs" as they were often heard to say. The most she would eat on any given Sunday were homemade rolls or biscuits and lemons, no matter how elaborate and tasteful the carefully prepared meals would be.

Finally, the entire Muse clan was there all decked out in their finest garments and acting in their best behavior. All my brothers, some visiting our church for the very first time, came along with their families. My four sisters, who were frequent visitors of the church, along with their families and friends were there. This of course, made me very proud to be their older brother, and my little girl was getting so much attention. Above all, however, mother was there, although she was very weak and frail, she somehow mustered up enough strength to come also. She was determined to be at Valerie's wedding even if it was the last thing that she did on this earth. Although she was so weak and exhausted that she collapsed immediately after the ceremony, and had to be treated by a nurse as she lay on a pew near the rear of the church, she never the less, made it through the entire affair. Little did we know that this would be the last public gathering that she would ever attend. And of course, as you may imagine, her presence meant the entire world to Valerie as well as the rest of the family. The next major family gathering would be for her funeral three months later, the first week of November, that same year.

The gala reception was held at the Auburn Hotel on the campus of the historical Auburn University. I often kidded her afterward by reminding her that I had even bought a hotel in the effort to get rid of her. Finally, with the wedding was over and everyone, as much as possible, set out to get back to normal. However, getting back to normal would become quite an evasive attainment during the next few months. For mother's condition would deteriorate to the point that she would become hospitalized more frequently, until her doctor finally decided that her being in the hospital would serve no useful purpose. She was therefore, dismissed to return home to die. Her doctor assured us that she was a proud and loving woman and that she would rather die with dignity at home than in the hospital. He strongly felt that she should die among family members whom he said, "evidently loved her so much, judging from the large crowds that filled her room throughout the times she was in the hospital." He also advised us that when the time came that we should not allow any attempt to resuscitate her, for such attempt would have no lasting results against the inevitable, and that she would not want that anyway, because she was such a proud and dignified woman.

My situation was worsened by the fact that Mamie would become hospitalized at the same time. She would have to undergo two life-threatening surgeries during the same time of mother's most serious illness. For more than a month I would spend my days at Mamie's bedside at the hospital until visiting hours were over, and then I would go by mother's house and sit with others siblings and friends of the family, who took turns sitting around the clock with her. This was my daily routine until Mamie was well enough to be dismissed from the hospital during the first time. However, a week later she would be rushed back to hospital for additional emergency surgery, which was far more severe than the first, taking in account her already weakened condition. Therefore, my daily routine was repeated for more than another week. The second operation proved successful and she was dismissed from the hospital. However, she had not recovered enough from the last operation to attend mother's funeral some ten to fifteen days later.

On an unseasonably warm and foggy early October morning, an unsurprising telephone call came from the Hospice nurse who was with mom during her final days, informing us that the life of this dear old lady, the matriarch of the Muse clan, had come to an end. I was not the least surprised for I knew before I left her house during the late hours the night before that she was lingering in her final hours with us. She died leaving in the wake of her passing scores of broken and hurting hearts and a vacant void in the lives of relatives, friends and acquaintances from over a vast area of this country, and especially throughout the greater Montgomery and surrounding area.

The painful day crept along amidst continued moments of heartaches and tears expressed by grieving family members throughout that awful day. By evening we had calmed down enough to come together to work on the funeral arrangements. At a set time, all the siblings along with some of their spouses came together and were assigned to specific committees that were responsible for investigating and gathering information for various aspects of the funeral. Some served on the grave committee and were responsible finding a suitable burial site. Some served on the funeral home committee, whose responsibility was to select a casket, the burial garment, arranging for the number of limousines needed to accommodate such large family as ours, and other such aspects that were handled directly by the funeral home. Others made up the religious service committee and were responsible the program for the funeral, which included contacting and notifying all persons who were to participate during the funeral celebration. The final committee was headed by a rather high ranking police officer who lived in the community, who assumed the responsibility of working out logistical plans and escort services throughout the city along the funeral route, from the home, the church and to the cemetery. He had volunteered his service as a way of showing his respect to mother and the family as a member of the community. Once the information had been gathered, we all came together again the next evening to share our findings, and finalize our plans for the funeral.

A brother-in-law, who worked part time at another funeral home in the city, headed the first committee reporting; in fact there were two brothers-in-law who did this kind of work. One worked on the, Internal Funeral Home Committee, while the other one worked on the, Grave Site Location Committee. Since the director of the funeral home handling our mother knew of their connections, he opted to sell us a-top of-the-line casket for a greatly reduced cost. He also included three stretched limousines instead of the two that came with our choice of plan, plus an extra hearse to transport the large volume of flowers that were already rapidly accumulating at the funeral parlor.

The next brother-in-law was over the Grave Site Location Committee. He had found a burial sight at the Oak Wood Cemetery Annex, which was adjoining the historic Oak Wood Cemetery in the northeastern section of Montgomery and is the oldest burial ground for the patriarchs of the city as well as for some foreign soldiers dating as far back as World War I, and many other aristocrats who may have lived in the surrounding areas. Most of the imposing grave markings were so old that they had long since turned black with age, and some were even leaning with time and erosion with lettering that was barely visible, even from the closest view.

The Annex is made famous by being the burial site for the legendary Hank Williams, the well-known country music recording singer whose spirited music thrilled our hearts many-a-days while we worked like slaves in the cotton field on the plantation. During those far off days I even found myself singing loudly and gleefully with him as he sang such songs as, "Hey Good Looking, What you got Cooking? How about cooking something up with me?" "Why Don't You Love Me Like You Use To Do? My hair's still curly and my eyes still blue, why don't you love me like you use to do?" His noted religious song "I Saw the Light" was indeed a great inspiration to me and the other children as young members of the church. While his lively singing literally thrilled our lonely hearts, it was mainly because in those days if we listened to radio at all we had to learn to tolerate country music, for blues and spirituals such as we sang were only aired in quarter hours blocks, only once or twice on any given day of the week.

Now Hank and mother will share the same cemetery, his grave located on the top of the hill and elegantly marked by an imposingly sculpted tombstone, and featuring a replica of his guitar, his western hat, his cowboy boots and chords of one of the songs that made him famous.

Mother's grave was to be located at the bottom of the hill only a few yards from the narrow well-traveled road that led to the top of the hill. Her grave would be marked by a simple grave slab with a low head stone and a lonely flower vase at the foot, in which the girls would place freshly cut or artificial flowers on certain days of the year, such as on Mother's Day, Christmas' her birthday and other holidays of meaning to them. Never before or since has such a large bundle of love and kindness final resting place been measured by such crude objects as a slab, a headstone and a flower vase, but mother, in her simple and un exaggerated modesty would not have had it any other way.

The committees reports continued, the girls worked on the, Dress and Makeup Committee, and were responsible for selecting the burial attire and makeup that they felt would be most appropriate for this grand home-going celebration. This was left entirely up to them since the rest of us had absolutely no knowledge or experience in this regard.

All this having been done it only left the formulating the funeral program and contacting the participants who were to appear on it. This, of course was not at all difficult for the rest of us since two of us were ministers and had pastored for a number of years, and therefore had much experience in assisting members of our churches whenever there were such needs among them. All these things having been done, the next challenge that lay before us was the funeral itself, which was set to take place four days later on the second day of November 1991.

A gentle autumn rain marked the morning of the funeral. It was scheduled for 11:00 A.M. By 9:30, however, the rain had ceased and the sun was shinning. Relatives and friend began to arrive at the home from different distant locations. Some muddled about the small crowded house while others sat in their vehicles or rested from their long trip sitting on the narrow front porch of the house, while they waited for the funeral hour.

The hour finally came for the entourage to load and depart for the church. The three family limousines had arrived from the funeral home that was handling the services. Also the funeral home for which my brothers-in-law worked part time, provided two more stretched limos as a courtesy to them, plus my dad brought long-time friends and family members from Orrville and Selma in a long limousine afforded him by the funeral home for which he worked part-time in the city of Selma some fifty miles away. Needless to say, our short street was not ready for such great surge of traffic, much less for the six stretched limousines that led the long funeral procession from the house to the church several city blocks away. When we arrived at the church none of us were prepared for the large number of people that had already gathered. In addition to the large number of members of mother's church, there were also unexpected buses from the churches that Nelson and I pastored in Auburn. Family members and friends of the family filled the small church to its capacity leaving the pulpit and the front of the church for the twenty or more visiting ministers and the truck load of flowers both of which stretched from wall to wall across the most sacred area of the crowded church. In the crowd sat several members of the local Hospice service, which, had faithfully attended to mother and the family during the most difficult and trying final hours of her life with us. For the first time we all realized just how consoling it is to be surrounded by so many sympathizing friends and acquaintances at such a time as this.

In less than an hour the funeral services were over, and the long procession trekked its way across busy streets and down long avenues, stretching many city blocks as it winded its way through the heart of down-town Montgomery where it skirted the snow-white state capital building immediately to our right as we made our way across town to the cemetery where mother would finally be laid to rest.

In our limo we could not help but discuss how happy and excited mother would be if she could see this great outpouring of friends and persons whose lives she had touched, near and far, in one way or the other, either herself or through some of her children or grandchildren before or after she had moved to Montgomery. She would find herself quite speechless if she was able to peer through the front windshield of the limo and observe all the attention that the motorcade was receiving from the local police department as they blocked streets and stood with their hand over their hearts as the hearse and the six stretched limousines briskly snaked by. However, she would be even more completely flabbergasted if she was able to glance through the rear windshield and observe the seemingly endless line of vehicles that stretched a mile or more in our wake. We could only imagine her wondering, but not saying, "You mean all this just for me, a single sharecropper mother from Orrville?" And with that she would repeat those most gratifying words we so often heard her say: "I am undoubtedly, the happiest mother and grandmother that can be found anywhere in this whole world."

After a brief graveside interment ceremony, the casket was lowered into the vault and carefully sealed amidst our unrestrained tears, our mournful cries and an aching void in our hearts that can never be filled. Afterwards, we boarded our cars to return to the church for an elaborate meal that was generously prepared and served by members and friends of the church and family, which signified that in spite of our woeful pain, and hurt, "life must go on."

During the next few months, things slowly began to settle in place. Mamie's complete recovery from her surgery and her return to her normal activities were indeed an answer to all of our prayers. Jimmy our youngest brother, continued to live in the house for several months after mom died. He later moved out and purchased his own home. The home house would eventually be sold and the very limited proceeds would be equally divided among the siblings. We were all sure that she would not have had it any other way. While we miss mom something awfully, we all managed to pick up the pieces and keep on living, still maintaining a strong bond as a devoted family unit even to this present time.

Chapter 19

From Instructor to President
The Pits of a Horrific and Unique Experience

I continued my teaching assignment at Selma University for more than a year after receiving the honorary degree. During which time I also joined a few other faculty and staff dissenters in seeking to present complaints to the Trustee board, which caused serious concerns and dissatisfaction at the school. Such as, to name a few: (1) The Board didn't seem to have the operation of the school at heart, and didn't have the slightest inkling as to what was going on in matters that were related to the on-going operations and needs of the school. (2) While they rushed to name new buildings going up on campus after themselves, they didn't have the slightest idea as to how the building and funding of these buildings had come about. This fact was made known to me one day as I attended one of the board sessions, when I heard the so called "most knowledgeable" member asked the question, "Brethren tell me, Just who owns Selma University? And just how are we getting so many new buildings put up on campus without knowing just how they have come about? Is this property placed under mortgage?" He concluded, "As a board we don't know anything." (3) We were also concerned about allegations that certain members of the board were waltzing into the business office and grabbing a fist full of money without even having to sign their name for it. It was believed that through this practice they were receiving more than the most tenured member of the faculty or staff, month after month. Of course I later witness this practice when I became president several months later. (4) Finally, we were concerned about the fact that a person of an entirely different religious persuasion was responsible to sign Religious degrees for Christian ministers graduating from the institution. Although we were branded as "rabble-rousers" and "troublemakers", we never the less, stood before them in a statewide meeting that was held at one of the local church in Selma, and voiced our grievances concerning these matters.

It was against this backdrop, that the level of my surprise was heightened, when I received a late night telephone from the president of our State convention, asking if I would serve as interim president of the institution, as the current president was resigning. I expressed to him that I would not accept this position for I didn't want to take the president's job. He insisted that I would not be taking his job because he had already resigned, feeling that the board was usurping his authority by bringing in a consultant team and assigning them over the overall day-to-day operations of the school, thereby making him a puppet president at best. He further stated that since we had raised so much concern about the operations of the school, that I would be viewed as a hypocrite having the opportunity to straighten them out and refusing to try to effect such change. He said,

"Furthermore, you can do more from the inside than you can from the outside." This having been said, I consented the greatest challenge of my adult life, to serve as Interim president of this one hundred plus year old college, one of several Historical Black Colleges and Universities (HBCU) having gained such recognition and located throughout these United States.

After serving as interim for a little more than a year I was appointed president by the board and served for four years in this very stressful, challenging and utterly impossible position. Progress in this position was made most difficult mainly due to the vast conflicts in philosophies and practices held by certain board members and myself as president of the institution. For instance, I was determined to put an end to the fluid access of certain members to the finances of the institution and their walking away with fistfuls of moneys to which they were not entitled. I also strongly protested an act of this same member for writing his name on an envelope and having it publicly announced as containing a certain amount of money, thirty five hundred dollars in fact, but having not even as much as one dime in it. While this was noticeably done by only one arch member of the board, all the members knew about it, or should have known, making them, as far as I was concerned, co-conspirators to this grossly unaccountable and unethical practice. Therefore, my very strong protest and opposition to these selfish and roguish acts made me a very unpopular and perhaps the most resented president that ever held that office. Since the most influential and oldest member of the board committed these acts, I knew that my days as president were numbered and that my tenure there would be an increasingly uphill struggle from start to finish.

Then there was the matter of the hired consultant that was in charge of the daily operation of the institution. He was responsible for the hiring and placement or replacement of personnel, the recruitment of students, and all the basic of operating the school, which made the president's position nothing more than a figure-head position. This of course was the case until I discovered that the consultant along with any number of his roving staff and workforce were just as unethical as and even more disrespectful than all the members of the board put together. I therefore, gave them an ultimatum, that either he or I would be leaving, for the both of us could not possibly be leaders of the university at the same time. Well, after making several unsuccessful adjustments, he left and I remained and set out to mold and re create the old spirit for which the school had maintained down through more than a hundred years. It had continuously maintained this unique mission and spirit until most recent years when it began to fall on hard times, as it failed to keep pace with the developments of most competing institutions of higher learning. Even among HBCUs. We were right near the very bottom rung of the ladder of upward mobility. Therefore, this noble and age old institution had become veiled in a garment of destitute, disgrace and utter hopelessness as far as I could see, and was indeed on its very last leg of survival as an institution of higher learning.

In an effort to curtail it's inevitable demise we set out to do the following: First, we set out to change the financial status of the institution by establishing an endowment, which up to now had never amounted to more than a one-time ten thousand dollar contribution that was given by a long-time president of our National Baptist Convention. Practically all the supporting Baptist churches of Alabama

236

that were sponsors of the university belonged to this convention. It was emphatically stipulated that these funds were only to be used as an endowment. However, in due time these funds too disappeared, never to be accounted for again even to this day.

My concern in establishing an endowment was prompted by a spirit of humiliation and embarrassment that gripped me as I attended a meeting of the thirteen private colleges and universities of Alabama, and viewing the statistical booklet of these institutions which included, among other important things, the schools enrollments, their area of specialization and their established endowments. While our university ranked right near the bottom in just about all areas, we were the only school listed in that booklet that had a zero endowment. And to make matters worse, we were sandwiched between two institutions whose names began with the same alphabet as our's.. One listed its endowment at seventy eight million dollars; while the other listed it's above forty eight million. It should not be in any way surprising that my embarrassment prompted me to set out to change this status, which not only should have been a prodding embarrassment to me as president, but to the board of trustees as well as all the Baptist churches, pastors, members and alumni that benefited from, or in any way lay claims to this age-old struggling and rapidly dying institution.

My attempt to rectify this destitute condition initially began at an annual meeting of the Alabama State Baptist Women's Convention, which is held on the campus in mid June of each year. I made copies of the aforementioned data and distributed it among the delegates attending this meeting. After pointing out to them the area of my concern and my sheer embarrassment as related to this matter. I also informed them of my sincere prayer that they deeply shared the same concern and embarrassment as I felt. I concluded, by telling them "this is the last time that this report will ever read this way, for as of this night, I am personally giving one thousand dollars which will always document the fact that we have at least that amount in our endowment." Several women in the audience, also pledged or paid one thousand dollars to match my modestly generous gift. Other smaller amounts were also given and even more pledges were made from attending delegates. That night, we raised more than six thousand dollars, with pledges of more to come within the next few days.

About the same time we received a memo from the United States Department of Education, indicating its interest in aiding Historical Black Colleges and Universities (HBCU) in establishing endowments and becoming acquainted with the practice of investing such funds to effect the greatest yield possible. The memo indicated that they would double the amount that we raised within a certain time frame. For instance, if we would raise one million dollars, they would give us two millions. We got busy writing our proposal for the grant. Realizing the difficulties of raising a larger sum of funds within the given time span, we set out to raise a more realistic amount of one hundred and fifty thousand dollars.

Through letter writing to pastors, churches of the convention, and businesses across the state, along with the alumni of the school, unnumbered telephone calls and countless face-to-face visitations, the campaign was finally on the way. Funds began to come in on a daily basis, and for the first time, making the receiving and the opening of the mail a rather delightful experience for me.

However, while most board members were very supportive in this effort, conspicuously missing on the actual contributor's list were this arch board member and the wing of the Alabama Baptist State Convention over which he presided as president, although he had publicly pledged to contribute twenty five thousand dollars from this wing. Any number of members of this wing did however, support with sizable contributions, but not as a wing of the convention as planned. This was the same board member who had previously turned in envelopes declaring that he had included a large amount of funds in it, and having his name loudly announced to the assembled audience, but having nothing at all therein.

Since the banks in Selma would not make loans to us at this time, we arranged to deposit our rapidly accumulating funds in a bank in the town of Marion, some twenty-five miles away, which was leaning toward helping us by granting us a loan. However this did not happen for this arch board member crossed us in a last minute attempt to make a much larger loan to cover a loan that he said he had made to the school some forty years earlier. Of course, such sudden change put our ability to proceed with the loan in limbo.

Believe it or not, when we were half way in our effort, the convention's president verbally guaranteed that if the board was permitted to borrow from these funds that he would be personally responsible to repay whatever amount they borrowed. Under this guise they borrowed some thirty thousand dollars from them promising to repaying it before the deadline date.

But in their very next board meeting they concluded that the president of the convention, who had made this offer, should not be held responsible to repay the loan as he had promised. Therefore no one could be held liable to replace it. This indeed was a very disturbing and discouraging development for me. We decided therefore, in order to prevent further recurrences of this practice, to transfer our funds to The First Tuskegee Bank, in Montgomery, some fifty miles in the opposite direction from Selma. This bank was rather accommodating to the school and gladly made us a sizable loan during a most desperate time for the institution. Already we had come to realize the impact that a sizable amount of funds can have in helping us to gain favors with such financial institutions.

As we neared the deadline date, and still had quite a bit more funds to raise, the convention's president turned against supporting the effort. He commenced by telling the pastors of the convention to send all monies to the convention's headquarters, and not to Selma University. He enforced his demand by telling them, "If you insist on sending your checks to the school rather than to headquarters, you keep them for we don't need them." Of course, this action set off an effort for us to seek the election of another president, which over a period of time we did. Needless to say I was caught right in the middle of that firestorm which didn't help matters very much so far as our relationship with him and the welfare of the school was concerned.)

The deadline date finally came. We had until four O'clock on Friday evening to get the agreed upon funds to the bank some fifty miles away for their official verification of the deposit. But we had one major problem, we were short by the thirty thousand dollars that the board had borrowed from the account, without which, our entire effort would have been in vain.

We were about to despair, when almost miraculously, one of the very concerned and highly influential member of the board appeared on the campus. He was to be commended for he had come from his home more than a hundred miles away, when there were others living right there in Selma, who never showed their faces on that day. He came straight to my office and asked if we had reached our goal? And upon learning that we were short by the thirty thousand dollars, he went to the phone and called the president. I overheard him telling him, "Mr. President, I don't know how you are going to do it, but you have got to replace that money that you and the board borrowed from those endowment funds. This president and the rest of us have worked too hard and long to miss this deadline." He further said, "It is now twelve O'clock, we will have to have it before two o'clock for it has to be in the bank in Montgomery for verification before closing time."

I don't know just how the president raised it so quickly, but by two o'clock we had the check. By two-thirty, the Bursar and I were speeding toward Montgomery. He filled out the deposit form while in route. Breaking all speed limits, we arrived at the bank just in time for them to prepare the necessary verification forms and wire it to Washington just minutes before the weekend closing of the United States Department Of Education, thereby beating the deadline just in the nick of time.

Three weeks later we received a check from them in this amount of three hundred thousand dollars, this gave us a total of four hundred and fifty thousand dollars in our once "zero" endowment. When I left the school a few months later this amount had grown to a total of four hundred and seventy-eight thousand dollars. Since then I have not had an interest in the activity regarding these funds. However, I assume that they are still in place and doing what an endowment is meant to do.

My Second greatest concern in the attempt to keep the institution alive was to regain our short-lived accreditation, which we had lost after several months of evaluation and self-study after having had a five-year accreditation by the Southern Accrediting Agency of Colleges and Schools. (S.A.C.S.) Selma University has been in operation for more than a hundred years, and has claimed great success in all of its areas of training. But, it has claimed accreditation for only a brief five- year period of that time, from 1991 to 1996.

Selma University was first a school for the training of ministers and Christian workers and educators. At a time it was both a high school and an institution of higher learning through the college level. Then it became a Junior College; and most recently it gained the shaky and forced recognition as a four-year college in all areas. This later status was added only after it had been accredited on somewhat of a trial basis as a Junior college for all academic courses, with only the Religious Department offering four years degrees. As of this writing, it has enjoyed this very brief period of only five years of accreditation by any regional accrediting agency in all its years of operation since it's founding in 1878.

During the former years the lack of accreditation didn't have such a hindering effect on the school in attracting students since it was located in the heart of the "Black Belt" area of central and western Alabama and was the foremost school of higher learning where blacks could attend in that vast area. However with the onslaught of integration there was competition with such schools as Auburn University; the University of Alabama; Livingston State, Troy State University and other more academic and financial affluence universities. These schools were drawing from the same pool of students and offering more scholarships, expanded choices and other incentives to them.

Selma University had now fallen on the worst of times, as maybe the case with most Historical Black Colleges and Universities. These schools are operating under boards that neither have the means nor the know-how to raise their schools to a competitive level with these invading competing institutions. This seems to be quite the norm for most of these age-old colleges and universities.

As brief as our period of accreditation was, it is without doubt that the loss of it was a near fatal blow to S.U. as far as attracting the better academic students was concerned. It was imperative and a matter of greatest priority for the institution, that the school regained its accredited status as soon as possible. Selma University even contested this loss by paying the sum of ten thousand dollars to appeal the decision of the agency, in a hearing that was held at their headquarters in Atlanta. This proved to be vain attempts to have them reconsider their decision. Even though we did have in place the endowment of four hundred and seventy plus thousand dollars. They still ignored our great progress and accomplishments over such short period of time. Their claim was that we did not have sufficient funds or plans in place to raise the necessary funds to adequately support the programs that we offered. They also stated that they had seen no evidence that we had raised the money that we claimed to have raised. The fact was that they had not asked for any evidence, therefore we didn't provide it for them.

Only one member of the Board of Appeal, Dr. Henry Ponder, a retired president of Fisk University, a significant HBCU in Nashville, Tennessee, argued in our behalf, stating that he saw a significant up-turn in our financial status in a very short period of time. He was even more vocal than our own lawyer who seemed to have been somewhat intimidated by the whole affair. Of course in the end, none of this did us any good as the agency seemed to have had made-up-minds from the outset and were determined not to change from their previous decision no matter how much evidence we may have presented to them. Realizing our sheer defeat in this effort, we boarded our vehicles and hurriedly return to Selma to map out further strategies as to how we could overcome this very serious setback in the life of our rapidly diminishing, but yet beloved old institution. By this time, we had already elected a new president for the convention. In fact, he had been elected shortly after we lost our accreditation. Therefore, he also accompanied us to the appeal hearings.

My next few anxious weeks were spent walking the floor most of the nights and sincerely praying for divine guidance for direction for what we should do in order to work through this over burdening problem. I further prayed that the Lord would touch the heart of someone somewhere that would be sympathetic to our cause and be willing to help us in this regard.

Within months the answer to my prayer came with an offer from a most unlikely source. In early January we received a call from none other than the former president of the agency with which we had been accredited. He was in his final months as president when we lost our accreditation and during our appeal process. He was also the long-time president of a very prestigious Ivy League and most financially endowed university in the state. His call was to invite us to a meeting that he wished to plan with our state conventions, both National and Southern Baptists; boards, Executive Secretaries from both conventions, along with boards of both schools; and or course, he and myself as presidents of both universities. Other influential members of the black and white conventions and community were also invited.

This meeting would take place over an elaborate luncheon, which he would host at his university on a near future date. When we had all gathered, he arranged for the two of us to sit together at the head of the table. As we were being served, he explained just why he had called us together. He began by calling our attention to the beautiful and elaborate campus, which housed exquisite classrooms, and imposing buildings that were second to none, regardless to the size and location of the university. He then informed us that all the buildings on the campus were all free of indebtedness, due to the generosity of their faithful alumni and supporters. He then assured us that he had no interest in acquiring Selma University as were often rumored by some of its older board members. He said, "because Selma University has made such lasting contributions to the people of Alabama and to the Baptist denomination throughout the nation, for such a long time, it would be a shame for all of us to just sit by and let this school close." He further stated that he wanted to help us, but in order to do this he said that we need to regain our accreditation, and that he wanted to help us to do this first, and afterward he would recommend us to some of his financial supporters with the assurance that they would help us. He even offered to make available to us as many technical assistants as we felt that we would need to help us in the development of the needed academic and social programs required by the accrediting agency. With that I realized that the Lord had answered my nightly prayers by laying our cause on the heart of someone that could help us in our insurmountable struggle for survival.

After the luncheon certain ones of us met together in a room provided for us at the request of the chairman of the board of Selma University, for a brief caucus meeting. In this meeting the chairman advised me to contact a very renowned retiring president of an H.B.C.U. His college was some fifty miles from Selma. He had been very helpful to us before. This time we were to seek his consultation in helping us formulate the necessary programs for the school and its surrounding communities, which would put us on track to regain our accreditation. After we had made several failed attempts to reach him by telephone, I finally was able to contact him, and we set a time for our committee to meet together at his school. As the time for the meeting drew near, my heart soared with excitement, for at long last it seemed to me that help for us was on the way.

When the set time came three weeks later, we traveled the fifty miles for the meeting with the president. Upon our arrival he introduced us to an African American gentleman, who was Academic Dean at another highly rated state supported university. He had been informed of our plight and was offering his assistance in guiding us through our academic and faculty preparation. The retiring president informed us of his intent to work with our board of trustee in the effort to forge them into the board that that they would have to become, if we were to turn the fate of our dear old school around and regain our accredited status.

He further stated that since we last talked that he had met several times with the president who wished to help us, and that he had shared an observation that he had gleamed from the luncheon that he had hosted in our interest several weeks earlier. He said that he observed that while Doctor Muse seems to vitally be interested in saving their school and turning it around, but that he was afraid that he could not say the same for the members of the Board of Trustees and the Baptist convention that owns it. He then said to me, "President Muse, unless we get a signed letter from you board verifying that they are willing to save Selma University at all cost, we will not waste our time in the effort to help you." With that statement he promptly dismissed the meeting, and we boarded our vehicles to return to Selma.

Upon our arrival at Selma, I immediately called the chairman and informed him as to what the president had said. He then instructed me to write this in the form of a letter addressed to him, and send copies to each board member, and wait for their reply. I asked him just why couldn't he just call the secretary of the board and have him write the letter that was needed to get this process under way? Of course, his reply to this was that he could not order the writing of such a letter, because each board member had his own opinion and that he could not anticipate just what their decision would be. Well as you probably have already guessed, eleven years later, I have not received one letter from any board member, not a telephone call or even a spoken word from any of them regarding this matter not even to this very day.

Rather than succumb in complete defeat, I then corralled the best minds of the school together to develop a program on our own. We worked almost around the clock, day and night with plans to have it ready for presentation to the board at its annual meeting the second week in April, - which is always held the day before the school celebrates its founder's day- about two months away. At the same time I was busily wording a letter of my resignation, since I was fully convinced that I could not depend on their support to restore or sustain the school, let alone to enable it to regain its critically needed accredited status.

The board meeting day finally came. The night before, we had set up screen and projector for the presentation of the projected program to them. When we arrived at the meeting the chairman commenced to state, " since this president and his staff has done such a good job, I, think that it will be in order for us to consider ways that we can give them a raise in pay." However, another member who said, "Mr. Chairman, you are talking about giving this president a raise, but I think that we should evaluate this president", immediately interrupted him. With that statement, the board immediately declared an "Executive Session" and I was dismissed from the meeting, without having the chance to present any part of the newly well-planned program to them at all.

At the end of our Founder's Day celebration the next day, the chairman of the board may a strong appeal for the board to reassemble, adding, "If you are truly interested in the future of the institution." Sometime well into the night as I had been asked to remain on campus until further notice, I was visited by the chairman and the school's attorney and was informed that the board had decided to discontinue all contracts of faculty and staff becoming effective before the month was over some three weeks later. He further stated that a skeleton crew will be renewed to handle the summer semester, and that mine would not be one of them. They both seemed to have been a bit surprised when I reached into the letter basket on my desk and handed them the newly prepared letter of resignation, as I informed them that had they let me stay in the meeting the day before, I could have saved them at least, one day of time while they were wrestling with the idea as to the best way to safely dismiss me without a possible lawsuit.

Their next question to me was, "since you understand the operation of the school, will you consider remaining on as a consultant to the upcoming interim president?" Struggling to maintain a certain level of Christian decency, I quickly responded that I had no intention of helping anyone do anything that they had not helped me to do while I pleaded to them for help over the past five years. Their next proposal to me was that I could remain on the teaching faculty since I was a tenured professor. I barked back, "what ever you want from me you had better get it by May 31st, for after that date so far as I am concerned, neither they nor Selma University will exist in any form whatever. I even refused to accept the honor banquet that they proposed to give for me, telling them to honor my predecessor instead. Of course this effort would have been in the attempt to shield from the pastors and supporters of the convention their evil scheme to dismiss me for reasons of which they have yet to make me aware.

With this I closed a most difficult chapter in my life, which was made even more difficult by the loss of my father who died during the first hour of January of 1996. He died without realizing that his prophesy had been fulfilled. He had uttered it when he first heard that I had been asked to serve as interim president of the school. He had stated, "Son, they will never let you save that school." I left Selma University a little more than one year after he died. And for the very first time in five years, I was able to sleep the whole night through and return to some previous level of personal sanity and with a clear conscience in that I had done all that I could to make a difference in this age-old institution.

#15. My photo as President of Selma
University 1994-1997

#155a. Article about the Selma University Inaugurations.

251

Chapter 20

The Founding of the Montgomery Bible Institute And Theological Center

Three months after leaving Selma University on May 31, 1997, I was led to open the religious school in Montgomery as I stated in my final report at the district convention.

I started the founding process in July of that year, which included pulling together a Board of Directors, locating a building for housing, filing the necessary incorporation papers in the office of the Secretary of State, and acquiring a non-profit business license from the city, and a license from the Alabama Department of Post Secondary Education, as well as buying furniture and equipment needed in the operation of the school. This process also included many other requirements and fees of which had I been aware, I probably would have had some second thoughts before venturing into this most adventuresome task.

Having everything in place, we were all set to begin classes by mid September of that same year. We were able to lease a building from a local Pentecostal church on one of the cities less traveled streets, for the amount of one thousand dollars a month, with the first payment due weeks before the signing of the lease. Of course, this was a seemingly insurmountable and impossible task, to say the least.

However, with the aide of a few sympathetic and supportive friends, churches and businesses who saw and shared my vision strongly enough to donate a thousand dollars or more each, to help us through the initial struggle, for we had no students or other source of income and bills were already pouring in, and had to be paid. Commemorative plaques were placed on the wall in the hall of the building showing that they were financial contributors toward the founding of the institution. Others contributed books for our library, which very soon contained a rather impressive number of books dealing with a variety of religious and even, some uniquely rare, cultural and other important subjects that were complimental to the courses that we were to offer, causing the small room designated for that purpose to seem rather full and complete making it the pride of our newly founded institution.

Getting the Word Out About the School

Our next move was to hold a prayer breakfast with pastors, local ministers and other religious leaders of the Montgomery area and surrounding churches, for after all, the public needed to know of our existence and what our mission was if we were to make a go of the school. Although the school is not designed to serve any particular denomination, most of the pastors and ministers attending the breakfast were from the local Baptist churches. While we had hoped that they would come out of an interest to see just how we could enhance their ministries and make for a more effective result in their preaching and leadership skills. However, many came purely out of curiosity, some to find out just what we were all about, while others only came for a meal that would cost them nothing. We also published an extensive write-up in the local newspaper, as well as sent notices to many of the local churches in the city and surrounding areas.

The breakfast had the opposite effect than intended, for instead of attracting persons to enroll with us, most of whom obviously lacked even the most basic religious and educational knowledge. Any number of the thirty-five or more persons left convinced that we indeed had organized this school to put their denominational school, Selma University out of business, even though Selma was some fifty miles away and most of them could hardly afford to go there anyway. This rumor had been started and perpetuated mostly by one of the pastors who just happened to be on the Board of Trustees of Selma University. I had clashed with him several times while I served as president and I was thoroughly convinced that his ignorance by far exceeded the high position that he was privileged to serve. More than any other, he could have greatly benefited by even the simplest and basic subjects that we were to offer, from English to Systematic Theology. Never the less, he too came to the breakfast that morning out of sheer curiosity as well as for the free meal that was offered them.

When the semester began several weeks later, we were fortunate to have had around twenty-five students to enroll for classes. They represented several different denomination and non-denominational churches in and around the greater Montgomery area. Even though I served as president, I was thrilled to be back in the classroom again working with those who needed my help so badly and appreciated the sacrifice that we made in order to help them. Other teachers were just as thrilled to volunteer their assistance with the teaching burden of the school. However, I taught most of the classes offered in both the morning and evening sessions. With this, we were finally on our way in the pursuit of becoming the best Theological school and Religious center with easy access to all potential students living in the immediate and surrounding areas. Through out the years we have even toyed with offering correspondence and on-line courses, however, due to strong competition and a very limited faculty and staff we had to table such plans until a more favorite time.

At the time of this writing, March 2008, we are celebrating eleven years in existence. We are very proud and thankful for our many accomplishments and innumerable experiences over the years, of which neither time nor space will allow even the mentioning of individually. However, I will take the liberty to mention a few of the rather significant ones, which I feel are most indispensable and very meaningful in the giving of a complete account of our experiences in the founding and maintaining of the institution since 1997:

During our second year we established an off campus site at our church in the city of Auburn, some fifty miles east of Montgomery. An associate minister of our church, Dr. Clifford E. Jones, who has also become pastor of The

Greater Peace Baptist Church, in Opelika, Alabama, one of the fastest growing churches in the state of Alabama, supervises this center. Between the students enrolled on campus and those enrolled at this site, we have amassed quite an impressive statistical success over the past eleven years, as forty students, some of whom were not even preachers when they first enrolled, are now pastors of rural and urban churches through out a vast area across the state.

During our third year as we searched for a place to relocate, we noticed a rather impressive and seemly well-kept building for sale on what was apparently the busiest boulevard of the city. While the street on which our school was presently located was one of the quietest in the city, this was without doubt, the busiest. At first I hesitated to contact the realtor to inquire about it for I was sure that it was priced far above the reach of our meager budget or our ability to in any way buy it. However, after passing by it for several months and noticing that the "For Sale" sign was still on its lawn at the prompting of my brother, I finally made the call. After several failed attempts to reach a representative of the company, we finally got a response.

The realtor met us at the site and after showing the building, he urged me to submit a bid and see just what would happen. He informed me that the building appraised for more than five hundred thousand dollars, but that I should make a bid that was suitable for the institution. After making a bid that was far too low, I finally, at the counsel of our board's chairman, increased it a bit and just waited for a decision from its owners.

After what seemed an eternity, we were informed that the owners had accepted our bid, and that they would sell us the building for one hundred and fifty thousand dollars, and that they would write off the balance of three hundred and fifty thousands as a gift to the institution.

Of course, I could not help but notice a parallel of these amounts and those around which we worked while trying to establish an endowment for Selma University. In that case, we were to raise one hundred and fifty thousand dollars, and the Department of Education would give us three hundred and fifty thousand dollars. In this case, we were to pay one hundred and fifty thousand dollars, and the owners gave us three hundred and fifty thousand dollars. May be by this act, the divine owner of all things was demonstrating his approval of the intense effort that we made and the tremendous sacrifice that seemed to have gone un appreciated while serving at Selma University.

One day as we waited for the approval of the mortgage loan, my daughter, Linda, who upon graduating from the University of Cincinnati, had moved back to Montgomery to help me with the operation of the school, said to me. "Daddy lets call the realtor and go over and dream over just what we can do once we are in the building." The entire building complex is a one-story brick and was built in three segments, (four with the "Bonus Room" included.) It spreads over a large area consisting of more than ten thousand five hundred feet. In order to go from one segment to the other it was necessary to enter from the outside entrance as internal accessibility from segment to segment was not possible. Therefore as we toured the property on this day, we were mapping out plans as just where to cut additional doors in order to obtain a feeling of continuity and making it serve as one building. Each segment, however, would continue to have its own sets of utilities meters, such as for gas, electricity and water, plus a rear entrance as well as the frontal.

Well, as it turned out, the usual representative was not available, so a different one came to give us access and to accompany us through the building. After he had walked us through what I always thought was the entire length and breadth of the building, he asked, "Dr. Muse, have you seen all of the building?" I replied, "Yes, I think I have." He informed me "there is an additional building attached to this one which has two additional addresses, and unless you have entered it from the side street or the rear parking lot, you have not seen it. This building is a part of the package that you are getting," he said. "We will see it now," he said.

We then exited the main building via the front entrance way and going down the side street to what I had thought was the rear of the building. We came to a ground-level porch that framed and gave access to a wide glass entrance encasing two glass doors over each were different addresses. Slowly he put the key into the lock of one of the doors, and opening it we walked in.

Boy! Were both Linda and I, along with a guest minister visiting with us that day from California, surprised? We were simply speechless with what we saw as we stepped upon dark green semi-plush carpet which covered the entire length and breadth the two sides into which the building was almost equally divided. Every inch of the walls were covered with elegant birch panel, and the white suspended ceiling on each side sported twelve wide-panel florescence lights with four additional panels in the luxurious executive offices that went with each side, as were the paneling and carpet that stretched throughout the building.

Even though the building was attached to the greater complex, it was never .the less, a stand-alone building having its own bathrooms, utility meters and the like and could be operated entirely independently of the rest of the complex. In dollars and cents, it alone was worth far more than what we had offered for the entire complex.

Trying to conceal my excitement, as we walked through the building, I mumbled to my guest minister, "Had I known that all this was included, my bid would have been much higher." He said to me "God knew that had you known about it you would have messed up the blessing that he is about to give you by over bidding. Therefore, He put blinders on your eyes so that you wouldn't know. Now they are honoring your bid, plus He is giving you a "Bonus, as well."

Once we closed the purchase, we named it, "The Bonus Room." We later added a door and built a ramp to connect the uneven floors making easy access between buildings thereby making the complex a complete whole. Several years later another door and a porch would be added to give that area convenient access to the vast wrought iron and brick enclosed parking facilities that goes along with the rest of the rolling complex.

After moving into the new facilities, furnishing and equipping classrooms and offices was our first priority. We therefore went about searching for new and used furniture at such places as Goodwill Industry, following up for sale ads in the local newspaper, and later on, purchasing tables, chairs, desks, computers and other such needed items from the State of Alabama Surplus department. These purchases enabled us to continue our classes, equip and make functional each office, host small banquets and other such gatherings, provide service to newly organized churches by serving them through our "New Church Incubation Ministry" program. From time to time through this ministry we have provided a meeting place for and given counsel to as many as four new churches that meet at least twice a week, on Sundays and certain weekdays throughout the year. At the same time, we encourage them to seek their own place in a community where their ministry is needed, as they do so other new start-up churches take their place here with us, thus the cycle is repeated over and over again.

Once in the new location, even with minimum advisertising, we noticed a significant increase in our enrollment. The stress of administration along with my teaching most classes became more than I could bear. I guess that in my excitement I literally over taxed myself, for by mid semester I had a heart attack, which had lasting consequences through out the entire institution. For as mild as it may have been, I found the attack to be very debilitating and energy draining for the next two years, forcing me to reduce my work load and rest in bed for long periods of time most days and especially on Sundays after I had preached a passionate sermon at church. I continued pastoring even during that time. During this time, our enrollment greatly decreased and still struggles today to regain the level of students that we lost at that time. Of course, my failing health made me realize that the school should not be centered on its founder no matter who he may happen to be. For, its cause, mission and reasons for existing are far greater than any human being can ever hope to be.

In addition my health problems, there were many other unexpected and insurmountable obstacles to be dealt with, such as repairs and replacing certain expensive appliances, repairing portions of the extensive roof that over the years had sprung leaks that threatened to damage walls and floors throughout the massive complex. Finally we had to build fences to secure the campus of the constant flow of undesirable traffic, both pedestrian and vehicular, that were always conveniently trespassing across our lawns and parking lot in the effort of bypassing the stop sign at the intersession just above our campus. This was done despite the posted signs warning against such action. All of this was very costly and most financially taxing, causing me to wonder if the opening of the school was indeed the "Calling of God" for me or was it some other cynical force designed to torture me beyond my limit of endurance. Whatever the case, I was in it for the long haul and determine to continue this mission all the way to the end of this life.

After eleven years of seemingly thankless toil and endless suffering and toil, we have realized many satisfying results and a great sense of fulfillment. The manifold and endless problems with which we are faced, have not weakened our determination to continue in the pursuit of our mission, which is preparing of Ministers of the Gospel, and other Christian teachers and witnesses to become the best equipped and the most effective preachers, teachers and witnesses of all times. To this end we are willing to pay even the ultimate price in this effort, thereby defeating, or at least not giving in to Satan, who opposes all good things and always seeks to overthrow everything that is intended to glorify the name of our Lord and Savior Jesus Christ.

MONTGOMERY ADVERTISER

LIFE
Religion

New Bible
training school
opens in
Montgomery

LIFE/1C

SATURDA

Dream comes to frui

Montgomery Bible Institute opens its doors to

The Rev. W.L. Moss, president and founder of the Montgomery Bible Institute and T
this new institute will fulfill the theological training needs of Montgomery-area studen

Registration for the spring semester at the Montgomery Bible
Institute and Theological Center, 4974 South Court St., will be Jan.
19.

Chapter 21

An Institutional Lynching at the County Courthouse

As with any college of higher learning it was necessary for us to partner or network with other institutions or agencies in order to offer services that were not exactly in our area of specialization. Therefore we were toying with the idea of offering computer training in order to familiarize our students and prepare them with basic skills in this field. We especially felt that ministerial student needed these skills for usage in the preparation of sermons and for performing other administrational work in the church.

Therefore Linda was very excited when she learned of ITEQ, Inc. a computer-training agency headed by a minority businesswoman. This we felt might be the answer to our long search for a partner in the technological training area. Although this company was based in the state of Florida, which caused some hesitation on my part, for, I had experienced quite a few problems dealing with out of state agencies while I was at Selma. I never the less, gave in and consented to go along with her recommendation to partner with them. After all, it was part of her responsibility to seek such programs as would enhance our statement of mission and provide some badly needed funds for the institution as well.

With the aid of a board member who was also a lawyer, the proper contractual document was drawn up and agreed on by both partners, and with that, we were in business, at least, I thought so. In a few days they shipped in at least ten desktop computers, textbooks, and a hired secretary to take care of their work, which was housed at the school. Our end of the contract was to provide the facilities for the program. Among other things, it was clearly pointed out in the contract that neither partner would be held accountable for discrepancies or problems created by the other.

All went well for several sessions. We were satisfied that in spite of my first apprehension, that we had indeed made an excellent choice in choosing to partner with ITEQ. And we were rather optimistic that this was just the program that we needed to take us to the next level and that it would soon equate with our already stabilized Religious Department. It didn't take very long, however, for us to discover that things were not just what they seemed. For more and more we realized that our partner was more interested in the money that her students were paying than she was in rendering satisfactory and qualitative service and training to them. Therefore service and training for the students grew worse and worse until it finally plunged to rock bottom. She even neglected to pay her teachers and staff worker and they finally quit and sought employment elsewhere. All this was after she had bilked the students out of some eleven thousand dollars each. And just as I had previously expected they would, ITEQ filed bankrupt.

This final downward spiral began when the owner of ITEQ, who was a lady of mixed racial background, brought a smooth talking Hispanic man by the office one day and informed me that he was from a national computer training cooperation named Bodercom, which is located in Miami, FL, and that he would be working with ITEQ in recruiting students for the program. She made it very clear that he would be working with her and not with us. While at the same time, she insisted that I would talk with him and inform him of just what I expected to accomplish through this working relationship. Among other things, I informed him that while the institution didn't have many resources we did indeed have a good name and that we were totally committed to protecting it at all cost, and that we expected the same of him if he was to work with our partner in fulfilling her end of our agreement. I further informed him of the agreement that we had between us such as: neither would make any public statement or announcement in the local newspaper without it having been reviewed and fully agreed on by both parties. It was also stipulated that neither party would be held responsible for any improper actions or faults brought on by the other. Although he appeared rather restless all the while we were in conference, he did verbally agree to all that I proposed to him. It didn't take very long however, for us to realize that he had absolutely no intention to comply with any part of the agreement. In short order he ran bogus ads in the local newspaper in the name of Montgomery Bible Institute, that ran for several days, promising students at least three thousand dollars for pocket money should they enroll in their computer program. He failed however, to inform them that this amount would be added to the loan of eleven thousand that they would be making with an out of town lending agency all of which had to be repaid in full on a monthly basis. Therefore since some students were seeking the so called free money provided by Keybank, they swallowed his plan hook line and sinker without even considering that they were being over charged and that in order for them to accomplish the level of training that was proposed to them they had to be far more committed to their study than they proved to have been. By the time we discovered the ad and had it discontinued, the damage was done. Once ITEQ got the check they broke all communication with us as well as with the students and their hired workers. We learned later that both companies had filed bankruptcy in the state of Florida. These developments left us in the legal cross fire and having to deal with at least three greedy and angry students and their lawyer in the Circuit Courts in the Montgomery county court house.

Of all the students that attended MBI, in any class, religious or nonreligious, the presence of these three students left me with an uneasy feeling from the start. Although I had casually conversed with only one of them during their attendance at the school, and neither time did we discuss school problems, mine was to offer some congratulations to him, as he was the only student who had passed at least two levels of the evaluation exam. I had absolutely no conversation with the other two at all. However I was aware of the fact that the other two displayed very poor scholastic ability and neither had passed any part of the exams. One wanted the instructor to accompany him in the testing room, which was in total violation to the rules of the testing agency. The other one very seldom came to class for he was always out of town, he even had an accident while visiting a girlfriend in Florida, which caused him to miss still more class sessions. Yet, on the day of the trial each swore under oath on the witness stand that they had conferred with me concerning the problems they were experiencing with their classes. Of course, I feel that they were prompted to lie by their unscrupulous lawyer who was desperately seeking to make a name for himself.

The day of the trial was quiet and uneventful with the exception of some dry-mouth feeling and torturing stomach butterflies, which were the result of my having to deal with the unfamiliar circumstances of having to be in court in the first place. On the other hand, there was the trepidation of being represented by a senior lawyer who had a heart of gold but was terribly lacking in courtroom skills, and who quite possibly had long since pasted his peak as a competent counselor especially in such a case as ours, thus leading me to feel defeated even before the trial began.

I could not help but notice that the students made a concerted effort not to sit in the waiting area where we were as we waited for the trial to begin; instead they stood aimlessly down the hall in front of the restroom area, or ambled restlessly up and down the hall making every effort to avoid entering into our presence. The most puzzling observation of all was the fact that neither the students nor their lawyer would look us directly in the eyes when we came face to face with them. This was a far cry from the way I had been taught and practiced all of my life, which is to look a man straight in the eyes whether he is friend or foe. Therefore their failing to do so was a clear sign to me that some untruthful and unethical scheme could be expected once the trial began.

The selecting of the jury was almost a mockery in itself, for the little defense lawyer almost demanded that any one who was religious and had the fear of God in their life be eliminated from the jury. While with our lawyer there seemed to make no difference for he had to ask for assistance from another lawyer to select the jurors that he chose.

Once the trial began, their lawyer stated his charges against us. Among other things he cited the charge of "fraud and breach of contract," He also clearly stated that he planned to shut the school down to prevent the practice of further fraud and deception. This he stated as he advised his clients as they testified under oath having sworn to "tell the truth the whole truth and nothing but the truth, so help me God." The evil scheme and greed of each of the three defendants was quite obvious as they responded to the question as to how much they thought that they should be awarded should the jury rule in their favor. The first student, who was the only white of the three, stated that he thought that he should be awarded at least $ 125,000. The next one stated that he thought that he should be awarded about the same amount citing his feeling that he should be given something for punitive damage he had received. While the last one stated that he thought that he should receive at least $ 50,000 for his trouble. Each of the students lied under oath that they thought that they were registered with the Montgomery Bible Institute, while they knew full well that they registered directly via a toll free telephone call with the company in Florida and that the only contact persons they met with at the school were employed by this company known as ITEQ. I for one am convinced that had they thought that they were enrolling in a Bible college for training in Computer Science, they never would have enrolled, and to enroll in Biblical studies was unthinkable and completely out of character for each of them so far as I could see.

The trial lasted a little more than a half-day. After a brief lunch recess, the lawyers made their final appeal to the jurors. The lawyer for the students, in a very poor attempt at drama, sought to close his argument by accusing me of being a Jim Jones and a David Coresh, declaring that the cyanide-laced cool aid would be forth coming. Our lawyer, on the other hand, only agued that we were good people who really should not have been on trial in the first place, but that we were the scape goat since ITEQ or Bordercom could not be brought to trial due to their having filed bankruptcy.

The jury however, seeing through their satanic scheme to exploit us and shut the institution down, awarded each student the sum of $20,000, instead of the more than $125,000, desired by two students and the $50,000, the other one felt that he should have been awarded. Even though they were awarded far less amounts than they desired, the $60,000, that we had to pay them just about dealt a fatal blow on the already struggling institution, which could barely afford funds to pay the ongoing mortgage and the necessary utilities bills from month to month.

In a desperate attempt to pay off the charges, we sought in vain to secure a loan by refinancing the building complex. The process took far too long leaving me to conclude that this particular bank was reluctant to loan us the funds. This decision was largely due to the fact that another member of our board along with me had personally assumed the responsibility to repay the loan. Each of us had a flawless credit record at the time and assets that were worth far more than the amount that we were trying to borrow. Our not being able to secure the loan coupled with the lowest ever enrollment in the school's history, sort of placed us in a very threatening position so far as meeting these financial obligations. In the meantime, the lawyer for the students became most desperate and sought to execute judgment against the institution by garnishing its bank account and seizing its property.

Their scheme to execute the sheerest form of torturous embarrassment and the most painful form of personal and institutional humiliation came of a Tuesday morning following the celebration of President's Day in February 2008. Having been made aware of their evil intent, I had gone by my lawyer's office to drop off an offer that I was somehow led to draw up during the night before. In this proposal I offered to personally pay the sum of $25,000, immediately and would pay the balance at such time as the newly applied for loan was in place, in forty five to sixty days. These funds would be drawn from a personal retirement fund, a convenient checking line of credit account, and funds from my personal checking account.

Worse came to worse before I arrived at work that morning, when I was informed by a staff member at the school, that their attorney had backed a rented truck to our front door and they were swarming like vultures throughout our building marking and loading computers and other properties which he intended to auction off in the attempt to collect the sixty thousand dollars they had through their lies been awarded by the jury. Of course they were accompanied by two deputies from the sheriff department who were very kind and considerate toward us, but had their job to do and that they did with much respect.

Their lawyer had left the school when I arrived but one of his workers reached him by cellular phone and gave me the opportunity to inform him of the proposal that our attorney was to present to him. Of course, I had no doubt that he would accept this offer, although at first he tried to play hardball by saying that he had to have all or none. However, once our lawyer came on the site he readily accepted, with the stipulation that the balance is paid in forty-five days. He threatened that if we didn't pay the complete amount by then that he would be back to seize the property.

They all sat restlessly around the premises for the greater part of the day waiting for me to drive a distance of more than a hundred miles roundtrip to pull the funds together. Just before four o'clock P.M. I delivered to them the money; they returned the broken computers and the other outdated equipment they had loaded back into the building from whence they had taken them, and then slowly slinked on their way into the night.

As you may know, the forty-five days came sooner than expected, when it came we were no closer to getting the balance than we were before. Therefore we were not surprised when we received notice from the lawyer stating his intent to return again to confiscate our property if we did not give him at least $15, 000. However, this was averted when two of our board members agreed to loan us $5,000 each, which he accepted and he agreed to hold off any further actions until the loan of the balance was secured. A few weeks later we were informed that the loan would not be granted due to our insufficient cash flow to sustain it. Thus we were back to the drawing board trying to come up with a payment plan that would be acceptable by both parties. If we can not come to an agreement we have no other alternative but to let them take the broken computers and the used office furniture that we had and then we will just sit back and see if they can satisfy this debt by auctioning them off.

The Saga of the Muses

Of course, the thought of this jarred my memories and took me back to my early childhood, when we witnessed the government break up farmers who were unable to pay on their loans due to the hard times brought on by the depression. As an eight-year old boy I couldn't for the life of me understand why the U.S. Government would take loads of starving livestock that were so poor and under nourished that their ribs and backbones were showing through their hides, along with these they also took old rusty and broken farming implements from several black families all because they couldn't pay their debts. In my mind, I can still see the trucks loaded with the property of these poor families, some sixty years later, as they filed pass our little shack of a schoolhouse. And now after all these years, I find myself faced with a very similar situation, as our broken computers and practically useless furniture will probably be loaded on some broken down rented truck to be sold to the highest bidder which will bring them far less than is needed to satisfy their judgment and greed. This gives credence to the old adage that says, "The more things change, the more they remain the same." If it is not the government that is doing us in, it may well be a Mr. X, or quite likely it will be one of our own people for whom many of us older people have sacrificed and some have even died in order that they might have a better chance at life than we had. On this note I take a temporary pause in this unending saga of life only to take it up at another time and place. This we do, not knowing just what course of action we must take to a more stress free future. We only know that we will do whatever we must in order to deny Satan the victory after all the Lord has done in blessing us all along the way.

Conclusion

There are those who ask, for what purpose is the writing this account of the life of a poor sharecropping family from Orrville, Alabama. Well, in the first place, in writing this retelling the writers hopes to document and share the life experiences of a seemly hopeless family who refused to be content with their lot in life and was determined to pursue the better life for themselves. It is also written in the hope that other such families who find themselves in a similar circumstance will be inspired to imitate this family and even exceed them in their own "Saga of life."

In the second place, the writer hopes to convey the fact that no matter the level of determination, life will be full of ups and downs wins and loses, and, that there is no such thing as "living happily ever after" unless the life span is very short and uneventful. However, without undying determination not very much will be done to bring about the necessary changes in the life of the individual or that of the family.

Thirdly, the writer reflects and high lights some of his inclinations, frustrations and disappointments that he experienced in his personal "Saga of life." Which at times were emotionally debilitating leaving him with the feeling of deep depression, loneliness and bitterness after having given so much in the effort to help our people and having received so little in return. Those that were helped the most are often the ones that exhibit the most thankless behavior and are the least likely to come to our aid at such time as this, when I need them the most.

Finally, while this account was not written for the purpose to obtain personal gain, we are making it available at a reasonable cost with all proceeds directed to the Foundation for the Support and Continuation of the Montgomery Bible Institute and Theological Center. In additional we welcome and prayerfully solicit such generous and heart felt contributions from such persons, churches, businesses and other organizations that might share our vision and wish to aid us in the continuation of this unending "Saga" of helpfulness by supporting us with your generous gifts. All gifts are tax exempt and may be sent to the following address:

The Foundation for the Support and Continuation of

The Montgomery Bible Institute and Theological Center

708 East South Boulevard

Montgomery, Alabama 36116

Montgomery Bible Institute & Theological Center
on 708 East South Boulevard Montgomery Alabama, 36116